MW00961833

Drugs of Abuse

Contents

WELCOME TO THE LATEST EDITION OF *DRUGS OF ABUSE*

The abuse of drugs is not a harmless personal decision: there are real, long-lasting, and devastating outcomes for those who abuse drugs and for their families, friends, and communities. And for some, the outcome may be lethal.

With the knowledge contained in this edition, you can make smart choices for yourself, and help others avoid the tragedy that inevitably comes from drug abuse and addiction. Whether you purchase drugs from a pharmacy, or you get them from a friend, knowing the truth about them will help you understand the dangers they pose.

Measured in American lives, health, safety, and resources, this cost is enormous:

» More young Americans die from drugs than suicides, firearms, or school violence;

» The use of illicit drugs, and the non-medical use of prescription drugs, directly led to the death of 38,000 Americans in 2006, nearly as many who died in automobile accidents;

» The only disease that affects more people than substance abuse in America today is heart disease;

» Substance abuse is the single largest contributor to crime in the United States;

» In the latest year measured, the direct cost of drug abuse was estimated at $52 billion, with indirect costs of $128 billion.

I believe none of this is necessary, and that with accurate, honest information about drugs, more Americans will make the right choices. *Drugs of Abuse* is designed to be a reliable resource on the most popularly abused drugs. This publication delivers clear, scientific information about drugs in a factual, straightforward way, combined with scores of precise photographs shot to scale. We believe that *Drugs of Abuse* fulfills an important educational need in our society.

Around the world and across the nation, the dedicated men and women of the DEA are working hard to investigate and arrest the traffickers of dangerous drugs, such as those described here. They help keep our schools and neighborhoods safe and secure. But just as important, they are working hard to educate America's youth, their parents, and their teachers about the very real dangers of illegal drugs. *Drugs of Abuse* is an important step in that direction.

Michele M. Leonhart
Administrator

II. Controlled Substances Act

CONTROLLING DRUGS OR OTHER SUBSTANCES THROUGH FORMAL SCHEDULING

The Controlled Substances Act (CSA) places all substances which were in some manner regulated under existing federal law into one of five schedules. This placement is based upon the substance's medical use, potential for abuse, and safety or dependence liability. The Act also provides a mechanism for substances to be controlled (added to or transferred between schedules) or decontrolled (removed from control). The procedure for these actions is found in Section 201 of the Act (21 U.S.C. § 811).

Proceedings to add, delete, or change the schedule of a drug or other substance may be initiated by the Drug Enforcement Administration (DEA), the Department of Health and Human Services (HHS), or by petition from any interested party, including:

» The manufacturer of a drug
» A medical society or association
» A pharmacy association
» A public interest group concerned with drug abuse
» A state or local government agency
» An individual citizen

When a petition is received by the DEA, the agency begins its own investigation of the drug. The DEA also may begin an investigation of a drug at any time based upon information received from law enforcement laboratories, state and local law enforcement and regulatory agencies, or other sources of information.

Once the DEA has collected the necessary data, the DEA Administrator, by authority of the Attorney General, requests from HHS a scientific and medical evaluation and recommendation as to whether the drug or other substance should be controlled or removed from control. This request is sent to the Assistant Secretary for Health of HHS.

The Assistant Secretary, by authority of the Secretary, compiles the information and transmits back to the DEA: a medical and scientific evaluation regarding the drug or other substance, a recommendation as to whether the drug should be controlled, and in what schedule it should be placed.

The medical and scientific evaluations are binding on the DEA with respect to scientific and medical matters and form a part of the scheduling decision.

Once the DEA has received the scientific and medical evaluation from HHS, the Administrator will evaluate all available data and make a final decision whether to propose that a drug or other substance should be removed or controlled and into which schedule it should be placed.

If a drug does not have a potential for abuse, it cannot be controlled. Although the term "potential for abuse" is not defined in the CSA, there is much discussion of the term in the legislative history of the Act. The following items are indicators that a drug or other substance has a potential for abuse:

(1) There is evidence that individuals are taking the drug or other substance in amounts sufficient to create a hazard to their health or to the safety of other individuals or to the community.

(2) There is significant diversion of the drug or other substance from legitimate drug channels.

(3) Individuals are taking the drug or other substance on their own initiative rather than on the basis of medical advice from a practitioner.

(4) The drug is a new drug so related in its action to a drug or other substance already listed as having a potential for abuse to make it likely that the drug will have the same potential for abuse as such drugs, thus making it reasonable to assume that there may be significant diversions from legitimate channels, significant use contrary to or without medical advice, or that it has a substantial capability of creating hazards to the health of the user or to the safety of the community. Of course, evidence

of actual abuse of a substance is indicative that a drug has a potential for abuse.

In determining into which schedule a drug or other substance should be placed, or whether a substance should be decontrolled or rescheduled, certain factors are required to be considered. These factors are listed in Section 201 (c), [21 U.S.C. § 811 (c)] of the CSA as follows:

(1) *The drug's actual or relative potential for abuse.*

(2) *Scientific evidence of the drug's pharmacological effect, if known.* The state of knowledge with respect to the effects of a specific drug is, of course, a major consideration. For example, it is vital to know whether or not a drug has a hallucinogenic effect if it is to be controlled due to that effect.

The best available knowledge of the pharmacological properties of a drug should be considered.

(3) *The state of current scientific knowledge regarding the substance.* Criteria (2) and (3) are closely related. However, (2) is primarily concerned with pharmacological effects and (3) deals with all scientific knowledge with respect to the substance.

(4) *Its history and current pattern of abuse.* To determine whether or not a drug should be controlled, it is important to know the pattern of abuse of that substance.

(5) *The scope, duration, and significance of abuse.* In evaluating existing abuse, the DEA Administrator must know not only the pattern of abuse, but whether the abuse is widespread.

(6) *What, if any, risk there is to the public health.* If a drug creates dangers to the public health, in addition to or because of its abuse potential, then these dangers must also be considered by the Administrator.

(7) *The drug's psychic or physiological dependence liability.* There must be an assessment of the extent to which a drug is physically addictive or psychologically habit forming.

(8) *Whether the substance is an immediate precursor of a substance already controlled.* The CSA allows inclusion of immediate precursors on this basis alone into the appropriate schedule and thus safeguards against possibilities of clandestine manufacture. After considering the above listed factors, the Administrator must make specific findings concerning the drug or other substance. This will determine into which schedule the drug or other substance will be placed. These schedules are established by the CSA. They are as follows:

Schedule I

» The drug or other substance has a high potential for abuse.
» The drug or other substance has no currently accepted medical use in treatment in the United States.
» There is a lack of accepted safety for use of the drug or other substance under medical supervision.
» Examples of Schedule I substances include heroin, gamma hydroxybutyric acid (GHB), lysergic acid diethylamide (LSD), marijuana, and methaqualone.

Schedule II

» The drug or other substance has a high potential for abuse.
» The drug or other substance has a currently accepted medical use in treatment in the United States or a currently accepted medical use with severe restrictions.
» Abuse of the drug or other substance may lead to severe psychological or physical dependence.
» Examples of Schedule II substances include morphine, phencyclidine (PCP), cocaine, methadone, hydrocodone, fentanyl, and methamphetamine.

Schedule III

» The drug or other substance has less potential for abuse than the drugs or other substances in Schedules I and II.
» The drug or other substance has a currently accepted medical use in treatment in the United States.
» Abuse of the drug or other substance may lead to moderate or low physical dependence or high psychological dependence.
» Anabolic steroids, codeine and hydrocodone products with aspirin or Tylenol®, and some barbiturates are examples of Schedule III substances.

Schedule IV

» The drug or other substance has a low potential for abuse relative to the drugs or other substances in Schedule III.
» The drug or other substance has a currently accepted medical use in treatment in the United States.
» Abuse of the drug or other substance may lead to limited physical dependence or psychological dependence relative to the drugs or other substances in Schedule III.
» Examples of drugs included in Schedule IV are alprazolam, clonazepam, and diazepam.

Schedule V

» The drug or other substance has a low potential for abuse relative to the drugs or other substances in Schedule IV.

» The drug or other substance has a currently accepted medical use in treatment in the United States.

» Abuse of the drug or other substances may lead to limited physical dependence or psychological dependence relative to the drugs or other substances in Schedule IV.

» Cough medicines with codeine are examples of Schedule V drugs.

When the DEA Administrator has determined that a drug or other substance should be controlled, decontrolled, or rescheduled, a proposal to take action is published in the Federal Register. The proposal invites all interested persons to file comments with the DEA and may also request a hearing with the DEA. If no hearing is requested, the DEA will evaluate all comments received and publish a final order in the Federal Register, controlling the drug as proposed or with modifications based upon the written comments filed. This order will set the effective dates for imposing the various requirements of the CSA.

If a hearing is requested, the DEA will enter into discussions with the party or parties requesting a hearing in an attempt to narrow the issue for litigation. If necessary, a hearing will then be held before an Administrative Law Judge. The judge will take evidence on factual issues and hear arguments on legal questions regarding the control of the drug. Depending on the scope and complexity of the issues, the hearing may be brief or quite extensive. The Administrative Law Judge, at the close of the hearing, prepares findings of fact and conclusions of law and a recommended decision that is submitted to the DEA Administrator. The DEA Administrator will review these documents, as well as the underlying material, and prepare his/her own findings of fact and conclusions of law (which may or may not be the same as those drafted by the Administrative Law Judge). The DEA Administrator then publishes a final order in the Federal Register either scheduling the drug or other substance or declining to do so.

Once the final order is published in the Federal Register, interested parties have 30 days to appeal to a U.S. Court of Appeals to challenge the order. Findings of fact by the Administrator are deemed conclusive if supported by "substantial evidence." The order imposing controls is not stayed during the appeal, however, unless so ordered by the Court.

Emergency or Temporary Scheduling

The CSA was amended by the Comprehensive Crime Control Act of 1984. This Act included a provision which allows the DEA Administrator to place a substance, on a temporary basis, into Schedule I, when necessary, to avoid an imminent hazard to the public safety.

This emergency scheduling authority permits the scheduling of a substance which is not currently controlled, is being abused, and is a risk to the public health while the formal rulemaking procedures described in the CSA are being conducted. This emergency scheduling applies only to substances with no accepted medical use.

A temporary scheduling order may be issued for one year with a possible extension of up to six months if formal scheduling procedures have been initiated. The notice of intent and order are published in the Federal Register, as are the proposals and orders for formal scheduling. [21 U.S.C. § 811 (h)]

Controlled Substance Analogues

A new class of substances was created by the Anti-Drug Abuse Act of 1986. Controlled substance analogues are substances that are not controlled substances, but may be found in illicit trafficking. They are structurally or pharmacologically similar to Schedule I or II controlled substances and have no legitimate medical use. A substance that meets the definition of a controlled substance analogue and is intended for human consumption is treated under the CSA as if it were a controlled substance in Schedule I. [21 U.S.C. § 802(32), 21 U.S.C. § 813]

International Treaty Obligations

United States treaty obligations may require that a drug or other substance be controlled under the CSA, or rescheduled if existing controls are less stringent than those required by a treaty. The procedures for these scheduling actions are found in Section 201 (d) of the Act. [21 U.S.C. § 811 (d)]

The United States is a party to the Single Convention on Narcotic Drugs of 1961, which was designed to establish effective control over international and domestic traffic in narcotics, coca leaf, cocaine, and cannabis. A second treaty, the Convention on Psychotropic Substances of 1971, which entered into force in 1976 and was ratified by Congress in 1980, is designed to establish comparable control over stimulants, depressants, and hallucinogens.

REGULATION

The CSA creates a closed system of distribution for controlled substances.

The cornerstone of this system is the registration of all those authorized by DEA to handle controlled substances. All individuals and firms that are registered are required to maintain complete and accurate inventories, and records of all transactions involving controlled substances, as well as security for the storage of controlled substances.

Registration

Any person who handles or intends to handle controlled substances must obtain a registration issued by DEA. A unique number is assigned to each legitimate handler of controlled drugs such as importer, exporter, manufacturer, distributor, hospital, pharmacy, practitioner, and researcher.

This number must be made available to the supplier by the customer prior to the purchase of a controlled substance. Thus, the opportunity for unauthorized transactions is greatly diminished.

Recordkeeping and Reporting

The CSA requires that complete and accurate records be kept of all quantities of controlled substances manufactured, purchased, and sold. Each substance must be inventoried every two years. Some limited exceptions to the recordkeeping requirements may apply to certain categories of registrants.

From these records it is possible to trace the flow of any drug from the time it is first imported or manufactured, through the distribution level, to the pharmacy or hospital that dispensed it, and then to the actual patient who received the drug. The mere existence of this requirement is sufficient to discourage many forms of diversion. It actually serves large drug corporations as an internal check to uncover diversion, such as pilferage by employees.

There is one distinction between scheduled items for record keeping requirements. Records for Schedule I and II drugs must be kept separate from all other records maintained by the registrant. Records for Schedule III, IV, and V substances must be kept in a "readily retrievable" form, or maintained separately from all other records.

Distribution

Maintaining records is required for distribution of a controlled substance from one manufacturer to another, from manufacturer to distributor, and from distributor to dispenser. In the case of Schedule I and II drugs, the supplier must have a special order form from the customer. This order form (DEA Form 222) is issued by DEA only to persons who are properly registered to handle Schedule I and II controlled substances.

The form is preprinted with the name and address of the customer. The drugs must be shipped to this name and address. The use of this form is a special reinforcement of the registration requirement; it ensures that only authorized individuals may obtain Schedule I and II drugs.

Controlled Substance Ordering System (CSOS) – Electronic Order Forms

Any registrant permitted to order Schedule II controlled substances may do so electronically via the DEA Controlled Substance Ordering System (CSOS). The use of electronic orders is optional; registrants may continue to issue orders on a paper DEA Form 222. CSOS allows for secure electronic transmission of controlled substance orders without the supporting paper DEA Form 222. The adoption of the CSOS standards is the only allowance for the electronic transmission of Schedule II controlled substance orders between controlled substance manufacturers, distributors, pharmacies, and other DEA authorized entities. CSOS uses Public Key Infrastructure (PKI) technology, which requires CSOS users to obtain a CSOS digital certificate for electronic ordering. The electronic orders must be signed using a digital signature issued by a Certification Authority (CA) operated by DEA.

Digital certificates can be obtained only by registrants and individuals granted power of attorney by registrants to sign orders. A registrant must appoint a CSOS coordinator who will serve as that registrant's recognized agent regarding issues pertaining to issuance of, revocation of, and changes to, digital certificates issued under that registrant's DEA registration. A CSOS digital certificate will be valid until the DEA registration under which it is issued expires or until the CSOS CA is notified that the certificate should be revoked. Certificates will be revoked if the certificate holder is no longer authorized to sign Schedule II orders for the registrant, if the information on which the certificate is based changes, or if the digital certificate used to sign electronic orders has been compromised, stolen, or lost.

Another benefit of the form is the special monitoring it permits. The form is issued in triplicate: the customer keeps one copy; two copies go to the supplier, who, after filling the order, keeps a copy and forwards the third copy to the nearest DEA office. For drugs in Schedules III, IV, and V, no order form is necessary. The supplier in each case, however, is under an obligation to verify the authenticity of the customer. The supplier is held fully accountable for any drugs that are shipped to a purchaser who does not have a valid registration. Manufacturers must submit periodic reports of the Schedule I and II controlled substances they produce in bulk and dosage forms.

They also report the manufactured quantity and form of each narcotic substance listed in Schedule III. Distributors of controlled substances must report the quantity and form of all their transactions of controlled drugs listed in Schedules I and II, narcotics listed in Schedule III, and GHB. Both manufacturers and distributors are required to provide reports of their annual inventories of these controlled substances. This data is entered into a system called the Automated Reports and Consolidated Orders System (ARCOS). It enables the DEA to monitor the distribution of controlled substances throughout the country, and to identify retail level registrants that receive unusual quantities of controlled substances.

Dispensing to Patients

The dispensing of a controlled substance is the delivery by a practitioner of the controlled substance to the ultimate user, who may be a patient or research subject. Special control mechanisms operate here as well. Schedule I drugs are those that have no currently accepted medical use in the United States; therefore, they may be used in the United States only in research situations. They generally are supplied by only a limited number of firms to properly registered and qualified researchers. Controlled substances may be dispensed by a practitioner by direct administration, by prescription, or by dispensing.

Records must be maintained by the practitioner of all dispensing of controlled substances and of certain administrations. The CSA does not require the practitioner to maintain copies of prescriptions, unless, such substances are prescribed in the course of maintenance or detoxification treatment of an individual. Certain states require the use of multiple-copy prescriptions for Schedule II and other specified controlled substances.

The determination to place drugs on prescription is within the jurisdiction of the FDA. Unlike other prescription drugs, however, controlled substances are subject to additional restrictions. Schedule II prescription orders must be written and signed by the practitioner; they may not be telephoned into the pharmacy except in an emergency. In addition, a prescription for a Schedule II drug may not be refilled. For Schedule III and IV drugs, the prescription order may be either written or oral (that is, by telephone to the pharmacy). In addition, the patient may (if authorized by the practitioner) have the prescription refilled up to five times and at anytime within six months from the date the prescription was issued.

Schedule V includes some prescription drugs and many narcotic preparations, including antitussives and antidiarrheals. Even here, however, the law imposes restrictions beyond those normally required for the over-the-counter sales; for example, the patient must be at least 18 years of age, must offer some form of identification, and have his or her name entered into a special log maintained by the pharmacist as part of a special record.

Electronic Prescriptions

On March 31, 2010, DEA published in the Federal Register the *Electronic Prescriptions for Controlled Substances* interim final rule which became effective June 1, 2010. The rule provides practitioners with the option of writing prescriptions for controlled substances electronically and also permits pharmacies to receive, dispense, and archive these electronic prescriptions.

Persons who wish to dispense controlled substances using electronic prescriptions must select software that meets the requirements of this rule. As of June 1, 2010, only those electronic applications that comply with all of DEA's requirements as set forth in 21 C.F.R. §1311 may be used to electronically create, transmit, receive/archive controlled substances prescriptions, and dispense controlled substances based on those prescriptions.

Ryan Haight Online Pharmacy Consumer Protection Act of 2008

On October 15, 2008, the President signed into law the *Ryan Haight Online Pharmacy Consumer Protection Act of 2008*, often referred to as the *Ryan Haight Act*. This law amends the CSA by adding a series of new regulatory requirements and criminal provisions designed to combat the proliferation of so-called "rogue Internet sites" that unlawfully dispense controlled substances by means of the Internet. The *Ryan Haight Act* applies to all controlled substances in all schedules. An online pharmacy is a person, entity, or Internet site, whether in the United States or abroad, that knowingly or intentionally delivers, distributes, or dispenses, or offers or attempts to deliver, distribute, or dispense, a controlled substance by means of the Internet.

This law became effective April 13, 2009. As of that date, it is illegal under federal law to deliver, distribute, or dispense a controlled substance by means of the Internet unless the online pharmacy holds a modification of DEA registration authorizing it to operate as an online pharmacy.

Quotas

DEA limits the quantity of Schedule I and II controlled substances that may be produced in the United States in any given calendar year. By utilizing available data on sales and inventories of these controlled substances, and taking into account estimates of drug usage provided by the FDA, the DEA establishes annual aggregate production quotas for Schedule I and II controlled substances.

The aggregate production quota is allocated among the various manufacturers who are registered to manufacture the specific drug. DEA also allocates the amount of bulk drug that may be procured by those companies that prepare the drug into dosage units.

Security

DEA registrants are required by regulation to maintain certain security for the storage and distribution of controlled substances. Manufacturers and distributors of Schedule I and II substances must store controlled substances in specially constructed vaults or highly rated safes, and maintain electronic security for all storage areas. Lesser physical security requirements apply to retail level registrants such as hospitals and pharmacies. All registrants are required to make every effort to ensure that controlled substances in their possession are not diverted into the illicit market. This requires operational as well as physical security. For example, registrants are responsible for ensuring that controlled substances are distributed only to other registrants that are authorized to receive them, or to legitimate patients.

Controlled Substance Theft or Significant Loss

Should a theft or significant loss of any controlled substance occur, a registrant must implement the following procedures within one business day of the discovery of the theft or loss.

A. Notify DEA and Local Police

The theft of controlled substances from a registrant is a criminal act and a source of diversion that requires notification to DEA.

A pharmacy must notify in writing the local DEA Diversion Field Office within one business day of discovery of a theft or significant loss of a controlled substance. Although not specifically required by federal law or regulations, the registrant should also notify local law enforcement and state regulatory agencies. Prompt notification to enforcement agencies will allow them to investigate the incident and prosecute those responsible for the diversion. If there is a question as to whether a theft has occurred or a loss is significant, a registrant should err on the side of caution and report it to DEA and local law enforcement authorities.

DEA must be notified directly. This requirement is not satisfied by reporting the theft or significant loss in any other manner. For example, a corporation which owns or operates multiple registered sites and wishes to channel all notifications through corporate management or any other internal department responsible for security, must still provide notice directly to DEA in writing within one business day upon discovery and keep a copy of that notice for its records. The notice must be signed by an authorized individual of the registrant.

B. Complete DEA Form 106

A pharmacy must also complete a DEA Form 106 (Report of Theft or Loss of Controlled Substances) which can be found online at www.DEAdiversion.usdoj.gov under the Quick Links section. The DEA Form 106 is used to document the actual circumstances of the theft or significant loss and the quantities of controlled substances involved. A paper version of the form may also be obtained by writing to the Drug Enforcement Administration. If completing the paper version, the pharmacy should send the original DEA Form 106 to the local DEA Diversion Field Office and keep a copy for its records.

PENALTIES

The CSA provides penalties for unlawful manufacturing, distribution, and dispensing of controlled substances. The penalties are basically determined by the schedule of the drug or other substance, and sometimes are specified by drug name, as in the case of marijuana. As the statute has been amended since its initial passage in 1970, the penalties have been altered by Congress. The following charts are an overview of the penalties for trafficking or unlawful distribution of controlled substances. This is not inclusive of the penalties provided under the CSA.

User Accountability/Personal Use Penalties

On November 19, 1988, Congress passed the Anti-Drug Abuse Act of 1988, P. L. 100-690. Two sections of this Act represent the U.S. Government's attempt to reduce drug abuse by dealing not just with the person who sells the Ilegal drug, but also with the person who buys it. The first new section is titled "User Accountability," and is codified at 21 U.S.C. § 862 and various sections of Title 42, U.S.C. The second involves "personal use amounts" of illegal drugs, and is codified at 21 U.S.C. § 844a.

User Accountability

The purpose of User Accountability is to not only make the public aware of the Federal Government's position on drug abuse, but to describe new programs intended to decrease drug abuse by holding drug abusers personally responsible for their illegal activities, and imposing civ l penalties on those who violate drug laws.

It is important to remember that these penalties are in addition to the criminal penalties drug abusers are already given, and do not replace those criminal penalties.

The new User Accountability programs call for more instruction in schools, kindergarten through senior high, to educate children on the dangers of drug abuse. These programs will include participation by students, parents, teachers, local businesses and the local, state, and Federal Government.

User Accountability also targets businesses interested in doing business with the Federal Government. This program requires those businesses to maintain a drug-free workplace, principally through educating employees on the dangers of drug abuse, and by informing employees of the penalties they face if they engage in illegal drug activity on company property. There is also a provision in the law that makes public housing projects drug-free by evicting those residents who allow their units to be used for illegal drug activity, and denies federal benefits, such as housing assistance and student loans, to individuals convicted of illegal drug activity. Depending on the offense, an individual may be prohibited from ever receiving any benefit provided by the Federal Government.

Personal Use Amounts

This section of the 1988 Act allows the government to punish minor drug offenders without giving the offender a criminal record if the offender is in possession of only a small amount of drugs. This law is designed to impact the "user" of illicit drugs, while simultaneously saving the government the costs of a full-blown criminal investigation. Under this section, the government has the option of imposing only a civil fine on individuals possessing only a small quantity of an illegal drug. Possession of this small quantity, identified as a "personal use amount," carries a civil fine of up to $10,000.

In determining the amount of the fine in a particular case, the drug offender's income and assets will be considered. This is accomplished through an administrative proceeding rather than a criminal trial, thus reducing the exposure of the offender to the entire criminal justice system, and reducing the costs to the offender and the government.

The value of this section is that it allows the government to punish a minor drug offender, gives the drug offender the opportunity to fully redeem himself or herself, and have all public record of the proceeding destroyed. If this was the drug offender's first offense, and the offender has paid all fines, can pass a drug test, and has not been convicted of a crime after three years, the offender can request that all proceedings be dismissed.

If the proceeding is dismissed, the drug offender can lawfully say he or she had never been prosecuted, either criminally or civilly, for a drug offense.

Congress has imposed two limitations on this section's use. It may not be used if (1) the drug offender has been previously convicted of a Federal or state drug offense; or (2) the offender has already been fined twice under this section.

DRUG SCHEDULING

This document is a general reference and not a comprehensive list. This list describes the basic or parent chemical and does not describe the salts, isomers and salts of isomers, esters, ethers and derivatives which may also be controlled substances.

SCHEDULE I

SUBSTANCE	DEA NUMBER	NARCOTIC	OTHER NAMES
1-(1-Phenylcyclohexyl)pyrrolidine	7458	N	PCPy, PHP, rolicyclidine
1-(2-Phenylethyl)-4-phenyl-4-acetoxypiperidine	9663	Y	PEPAP, synthetic heroin
1-[1-(2-Thienyl)cyclohexyl]piperidine	7470	N	TCP, tenocyclidine
1-[1-(2-Thienyl)cyclohexyl]pyrrolidine	7473	N	TCPy
1-Methyl-4-phenyl-4-propionoxypiperidine	9661	Y	MPPP, synthetic heroin
2,5-Dimethoxy-4-(n)-propylthiophenethylamine	7348	N	2C-t-7
2,5-Dimethoxy-4-ethylamphetamine	7399	N	DOET
2,5-Dimethoxyamphetamine	7396	N	DMA, 2,5-DMA
3,4,5-Trimethoxyamphetamine	7390	N	TMA
3,4-Methylenedioxyamphetamine	7400	N	MDA, Love Drug
3,4-Methylenedioxymethamphetamine	7405	N	MDMA, Ecstasy, XTC
3,4-Methylenedioxy-N-ethylamphetamine	7404	N	N-ethyl MDA, MDE, MDEA
3-Methylfentanyl	9813	Y	China White, fentanyl
3-Methylthiofentanyl	9833	Y	China White, fentanyl
4-Bromo-2,5-dimethoxyamphetamine	7391	N	DOB, 4-bromo-DMA
4-Bromo-2,5-dimethoxyphenethylamine	7392	N	Nexus, 2-CB, has been sold as Ecstasy, i.e. MDMA
4-Methoxyamphetamine	7411	N	PMA
4-Methyl-2,5-dimethoxyamphetamine	7395	N	DOM, STP
4-Methylaminorex (cis isomer)	1590	N	U4Euh, McN-422
5-Methoxy-3,4-methylenedioxyamphetamine	7401	N	MMDA
5-Methoxy-N,N-diisopropyltryptamine	7439	N	5-MeO-DIPT
Acetorphine	9319	Y	
Acetyl-alpha-methylfentanyl	9815	Y	
Acetyldihydrocodeine	9051	Y	Acetylcodone
Acetylmethadol	9601	Y	Methadyl acetate
Allylprodine	9602	Y	
Alphacetylmethadol except levo-alphacetylmethadol	9603	Y	
Alpha-Ethyltryptamine	7249	N	ET, Trip
Alphameprodine	9604	Y	
Alphamethadol	9605	Y	
Alpha-Methylfentanyl	9814	Y	China White, fentanyl
Alpha-Methylthiofentanyl	9832	Y	China White, fentanyl
Alpha-methyltryptamine	7432	N	AMT
Aminorex	1585	N	has been sold as methamphetamine
Benzethidine	9606	Y	
Benzylmorphine	9052	Y	
Betacetylmethadol	9607	Y	

SCHEDULE I

SUBSTANCE	DEA NUMBER	NARCOTIC	OTHER NAMES
Beta-hydroxy-3-methylfentanyl	9831	Y	China White, fentanyl
Beta-hydroxyfentanyl	9830	Y	China White, fentanyl
Betameprodine	9608	Y	
Betamethadol	9609	Y	
Betaprodine	9611	Y	
Bufotenine	7433	N	Mappine, N,N-dimethylserotonin
Cathinone	1235	N	Constituent of "Khat" plant
Clonitazene	9612	Y	
Codeine methylbromide	9070	Y	
Codeine-N-oxide	9053	Y	
Cyprenorphine	9054	Y	
Desomorphine	9055	Y	
Dextromoramide	9613	Y	Palfium, Jetrium, Narcolo
Diampromide	9615	Y	
Diethylthiambutene	9616	Y	
Diethyltryptamine	7434	N	DET
Difenoxin	9168	Y	Lyspafen
Dihydromorphine	9145	Y	
Dimenoxadol	9617	Y	
Dimepheptanol	9618	Y	
Dimethylthiambutene	9619	Y	
Dimethyltryptamine	7435	N	DMT
Dioxaphetyl butyrate	9621	Y	
Dipipanone	9622	Y	Dipipan, phenylpiperone HCl, Diconal, Wellconal
Drotebanol	9335	Y	Metebanyl, oxymethebanol
Ethylmethylthiambutene	9623	Y	
Etonitazene	9624	Y	
Etorphine (except HCl)	9056	Y	
Etoxeridine	9625	Y	
Fenethylline	1503	N	Captagon, amfetyline, ethyltheophylline amphetamine
Furethidine	9626	Y	
Gama Hydroxybutyric Acid	2010	N	GHB, gama hydroxybutyrate, sodium oxybate
Heroin	9200	Y	Diacetylmorphine, diamorphine
Hydromorphinol	9301	Y	
Hydroxypethidine	9627	Y	
Ibogaine	7260	N	Constituent of "Tabernanthe iboga" plant
Ketobemidone	9628	Y	Cliradon
Levomoramide	9629	Y	
Levophenacylmorphan	9631	Y	
Lysergic acid diethylamide	7315	N	LSD, lysergide

SCHEDULE I

SUBSTANCE	DEA NUMBER	NARCOTIC	OTHER NAMES
Marijuana	7360	N	Cannabis, marijuana
Mecloqualone	2572	N	Nubarene
Mescaline	7381	N	Constituent of "Peyote" cacti
Methaqualone	2565	N	Quaalude, Parest, Somnafac, Opitimil, Mandrax
Methcathinone	1237	N	N-Methylcathinone, "cat"
Methyldesorphine	9302	Y	
Methyldihydromorphine	9304	Y	
Morpheridine	9632	Y	
Morphine methylbromide	9305	Y	
Morphine methylsulfonate	9306	Y	
Morphine-N-oxide	9307	Y	
Myrophine	9308	Y	
N,N-Dimethylamphetamine	1480	N	
N-Benzylpiperazine	7493	N	BZP, 1-benzylpiperazine
N-Ethyl-1-phenylcyclohexylamine	7455	N	PCE
N-Ethyl-3-piperidyl benzilate	7482	N	JB 323
N-Ethylamphetamine	1475	N	NEA
N-Hydroxy-3,4-methylenedioxyamphetamine	7402	N	N-hydroxy MDA
Nicocodeine	9309	Y	
Nicomorphine	9312	Y	Vilan
N-Methyl-3-piperidyl benzilate	7484	N	JB 336
Noracymethadol	9633	Y	
Norlevorphanol	9634	Y	
Normethadone	9635	Y	Phenyldimazone
Normorphine	9313	Y	
Norpipanone	9636	Y	
Para-Fluorofentanyl	9812	Y	China White, fentanyl
Parahexyl	7374	N	Synhexyl,
Peyote	7415	N	Cactus which contains mescaline
Phenadoxone	9637	Y	
Phenampromide	9638	Y	
Phenomorphan	9647	Y	
Phenoperidine	9641	Y	Operidine, Lealgin
Pholcodine	9314	Y	Copholco, Adaphol, Codisol, Lantuss, Pholcolin
Piritramide	9642	Y	Piridolan
Proheptazine	9643	Y	
Properidine	9644	Y	
Propiram	9649	Y	Algeril
Psilocybin	7437	N	Constituent of "Magic mushrooms"
Psilocyn	7438	N	Psilocin, constituent of "Magic mushrooms"

SCHEDULE I

SUBSTANCE	DEA NUMBER	NARCOTIC	OTHER NAMES
Racemoramide	9645	Y	
Tetrahydrocannabinols	7370	N	THC, Delta-8 THC, Delta-9 THC, dronabinol and others
Thebacon	9315	Y	Acetylhydrocodone, Acedicon, Thebacetyl
Thiofentanyl	9835	Y	Chine white, fentanyl
Tilidine	9750	Y	Tilidate, Valoron, Kitadol, Lak, Tilsa
Trimeperidine	9646	Y	Promedolum

SCHEDULE II

SUBSTANCE	DEA NUMBER	NARCOTIC	OTHER NAMES
1-Phenylcyclohexylamine	7460	N	Precursor of PCP
1-Piperidinocyclohexanecarbonitrile	8603	N	PCC, precursor of PCP
4-Anilino-N-phenethyl-4-piperidine (ANPP)	8333	N	ANPP
Alfentanil	9737	Y	Alfenta
Alphaprodine	9010	Y	Nisentil
Amobarbital	2125	N	Amytal, Tuinal
Amphetamine	1100	N	Dexedrine, Adderall, Obetrol
Anileridine	9020	Y	Leritine
Benzoylecgonine	9180	Y	Cocaine metabolite
Bezitramide	9800	Y	Burgodin
Carfentanil	9743	Y	Wildnil
Coca Leaves	9040	Y	
Cocaine	9041	Y	Methyl benzoylecgonine, Crack
Codeine	9050	Y	Morphine methyl ester, methyl morphine
Dextropropoxyphene, bulk (non-dosage forms)	9273	Y	Propoxyphene
Dihydrocodeine	9120	Y	Didrate, Parzone
Dihydroetorphine	9334	Y	DHE
Diphenoxylate	9170	Y	
Diprenorphine	9058	Y	M50-50
Ecgonine	9180	Y	Cocaine precursor, in Coca leaves
Ethylmorphine	9190	Y	Dionin
Etorphine	9059	Y	M 99
Fentanyl	9801	Y	Duragesic, Oralet, Actiq, Sublimaze, Innovar
Glutethimide	2550	N	Doriden, Dorimide
Hydrocodone	9193	Y	dihydrocodeinone
Hydromorphone	9150	Y	Dilaudid, dihydromorphinone
Isomethadone	9226	Y	Isoamidone
Levo-alphacetylmethadol	9648	Y	LAAM, long acting methadone, levomethadyl acetate

SCHEDULE II

SUBSTANCE	DEA NUMBER	NARCOTIC	OTHER NAMES
Levomethorphan	9210	Y	
Levorphanol	9220	Y	Levo-Dromoran
Lisdexamfetamine	1205	N	Vyvans
Meperidine	9230	Y	Demerol, Mepergan, pethidine
Meperidine intermediate-A	9232	Y	Meperidine precursor
Meperidine intermediate-B	9233	Y	Meperidine precursor, normeperidine
Meperidine intermediate-C	9234	Y	Meperidine precursor
Metazocine	9240	Y	
Methadone	9250	Y	Dolophine, Methadose, Amidone
Methadone intermediate	9254	Y	Methadone precursor
Methamphetamine	1105	N	Desoxyn, D-desoxyephedrine, ICE, Crank, Speed
Methylphenidate	1724	N	Concerta, Ritalin, Methylin
Metopon	9260	Y	
Moramide-intermediate	9802	Y	
Morphine	9300	Y	MS Contin, Roxanol, Oramorph, RMS, MSIR
Nabilone	7379	N	Cesamet
Opium extracts	9610	Y	
Opium fluid extract	9620	Y	
Opium poppy	9650	Y	Papaver somniferum
Opium tincture	9630	Y	Laudanum
Opium, granulated	9640	Y	Granulated opium
Opium, powdered	9639	Y	Powdered Opium
Opium, raw	9600	Y	Raw opium, gum opium
Oripavine	9330	Y	
Oxycodone	9143	Y	OxyContin, Percocet, Endocet, Roxicodone, Roxicet
Oxymorphone	9652	Y	Numorphan
Pentobarbital	2270	N	Nembutal
Phenazocine	9715	Y	Narphen, Prinadol
Phencyclidine	7471	N	PCP, Sernylan
Phenmetrazine	1631	N	Preludin
Phenylacetone	8501	N	P2P, phenyl-2-propanone, benzyl methyl ketone
Piminodine	9730	Y	
Poppy Straw	9650	Y	Opium poppy capsules, poppy heads
Poppy Straw Concentrate	9670	Y	Concentrate of Poppy Straw, CPS
Racemethorphan	9732	Y	
Racemorphan	9733	Y	Dromoran
Remifentanil	9739	Y	Ultiva
Secobarbital	2315	N	Seconal, Tuinal
Sufentanil	9740	Y	Sufenta
Tapentadol	9780	Y	
Thebaine	9333	Y	Precursor of many narcotics

SCHEDULE III

SUBSTANCE	DEA NUMBER	NARCOTIC	OTHER NAMES
13Beta-ethyl-17beta-hydroxygon-4-en-3-one	4000	N	
17Alpha-methyl-3alpha,17beta-dihydroxy-5alphaandrostane	4000	N	
17Alpha-methyl-3beta,17beta-dihydroxy-5alphaandrostane	4000	N	
17Alpha-methyl-3beta,17beta-dihydroxyandrost-4-ene	4000	N	
17Alpha-methyl-4-hydroxynandrolone (17alpha-methyl-4-hydroxy-17beta-hydroxyestr-4-en-3-one)	4000	N	
17Alpha-methyl-delta1-dihydrotestosterone (17beta-hydroxy-17alpha-methyl-5alpha-androst-1-en-3-one)	4000	N	17-Alpha-methyl-1-testosterone
19-Nor-4,9(10)-androstadienedione	4000	N	
19-Nor-4-androstenediol (3beta,17beta-dihydroxyestr-4-ene; 3alpha,17beta-dihydroxyestr-4-ene)	4000	N	
19-Nor-4-androstenedione (estr-4-en-3,17-dione) 4000 III N	4000	N	
19-Nor-5-androstenediol (3beta,17beta-dihydroxyestr-5-ene; 3alpha,17beta-dihydroxyestr-5-ene)	4000	N	
19-Nor-5-androstenedione (estr-5-en-3,17-dione)	4000	N	
1-Androstenediol (3beta,17beta-dihydroxy-5alphaandrost-1-ene; 3alpha,17beta-dihydroxy-5alphaandrost-1-ene)	4000	N	
1-Androstenedione (5alpha-androst-1-en-3,17-dione)	4000	N	
3Alpha,17beta-dihydroxy-5alpha-androstane	4000	N	
3Beta,17beta-dihydroxy-5alpha-androstane	4000	N	
4-Androstenediol (3beta,17beta-dihydroxy-androst-4-ene)	4000	N	4-AD
4-Androstenedione (androst-4-en-3,17-dione)	4000	N	
4-Dihydrotestosterone (17beta-hydroxyandrostan-3-one)	4000	N	Anabolex, Andractim, Pesomax, Stanolone
4-Hydroxy-19-nortestosterone (4,17beta-dihydroxyestr-4-en-3-one)	4000	N	
4-Hydroxytestosterone (4,17beta-dihydroxyandrost-4-en-3-one)	4000	N	
5-Androstenediol (3beta,17beta-dihydroxy-androst-5-ene)	4000	N	
5-Androstenedione (androst-5-en-3,17-dione)	4000	N	
Amobarbital & noncontrolled active ingred.	2126	N	
Amobarbital suppository dosage form	2126	N	
Anabolic steroids	4000	N	Body Building drugs
Androstanedione (5alpha-androstan-3,17-dione)	4000	N	
Aprobarbital	2100	N	Alurate
Barbituric acid derivative	2100	N	Barbiturates not specifically listed
Benzphetamine	1228	N	Didrex, Inapetyl
Bolasterone (7alpha,17alpha-dimethyl-17beta-hydroxyandrost-4-en-3-one)	4000	N	
Boldenone (17beta-hydroxyandrost-1,4-diene-3-one)	4000	N	Equipoise, Parenabol, Vebonol, dehydrotestosterone
Boldione	4000	N	
Buprenorphine	9064	Y	Buprenex, Temgesic, Subutex, Suboxone
Butabarbital (secbutabarbital)	2100	N	Butisol, Butibel
Butalbital	2100	N	Fiorinal, Butalbital with aspirin

SCHEDULE III

SUBSTANCE	DEA NUMBER	NARCOTIC	OTHER NAMES
Butobarbital (butethal)	2100	N	Soneryl (UK)
Calusterone (7beta,17alpha-dimethyl-17betahydroxyandrost-4-en-3-one)	4000	N	Methosarb
Chlorhexadol	2510	N	Mechloral, Mecoral, Medodorm, Chloralodol
Chlorphentermine	1645	N	Pre-Sate, Lucofen, Apsedon, Desopimon
Clortermine	1647	N	Voranil
Clostebol (4-chloro-17beta-hydroxyandrost-4-en-3-one)	4000	N	Alfa-Trofodermin, Clostene, 4-chlorotestosterone
Codeine & isoquinoline alkaloid 90 mg/du	9803	Y	Codeine with papaverine or noscapine
Codeine combination product 90 mg/du	9804	Y	Empirin,Fiorinal,Tylenol,ASA or APAP w/ codeine
Dehydrochloromethyltestosterone (4-chloro-17betahydroxy-17alpha-methylandrost-1,4-dien-3-one)	4000	N	Oral-Turinabol
Delta1-dihydrotestosterone (17beta-hydroxy-5alphaandrost-1-en-3-one)	4000	N	1-Testosterone
Desoxymethyltestosterone	4000	N	
Dihydrocodeine combination product 90 mg/du	9807	Y	Synalgos-DC, Compal
Dronabinol (synthetic) in sesame oil in soft gelatin capsule as approved by FDA	7369	N	Marinol, synthetic THC in sesame oil/soft gelatin as approved by FDA
Drostanolone (17beta-hydroxy-2alpha-methyl-5alphaandrostan-3-one)	4000	N	Drolban, Masterid, Permastril
Embutramide	2020	N	Tributane
Ethylestrenol (17alpha-ethyl-17beta-hydroxyestr-4-ene)	4000	N	Maxibolin, Orabolin, Durabolin-O, Duraboral
Ethylmorphine combination product 15 mg/du	9808	Y	
Fluoxymesterone (9-fluoro-17alpha-methyl-11beta, 17beta-dihydroxyandrost-4-en-3-one)	4000	N	Anadroid-F, Halotestin, Ora-Testryl
Formebolone (2-formyl-17alpha-methyl-11alpha, 17beta-dihydroxyandrost-1,4-dien-3-one)	4000	N	Esiclene, Hubernol
Furazabol (17alpha-methyl-17betahydroxyandrostano[2,3-c]-furazan)	4000	N	Frazalon, Miotolon, Qu Zhi Shu
Gamma Hydroxybutyric Acid preparations	2012	N	Xyrem
Hydrocodone & isoquinoline alkaloid <15 mg/du	9805	Y	Dihydrocodeinone+papaverine or noscapine
Hydrocodone combination product <15 mg/du	9806	Y	Lorcet, Lortab,Vicodin, Vicoprofen,Tussionex, Norco
Ketamine	7285	N	Ketaset, Ketalar, Special K, K
Lysergic acid	7300	N	LSD precursor
Lysergic acid amide	7310	N	LSD precursor
Mestanolone (17alpha-methyl-17beta-hydroxy-5alphaandrostan-3-one)	4000	N	Assimil, Ermalone, Methybol, Tantarone
Mesterolone (1alpha-methyl-17beta-hydroxy-5alphaandrostan-3-one)	4000	N	Androviron, Proviron, Testiwop
Methandienone (17alpha-methyl-17betahydroxyandrost-1, 4-diene-3-one)	4000	N	Dianabol, Metabolina, Nerobol, Perbolin
Methandriol (17alpha-methyl-3beta, 17betadihydroxyandrost-5-ene)	4000	N	Sinesex, Stenediol, Troformone

SCHEDULE III

SUBSTANCE	DEA NUMBER	NARCOTIC	OTHER NAMES
Methenolone (1-methyl-17beta-hydroxy-5alpha-androst-1-en-3-one)	4000	N	Primobolan, Primobolan Depot, Primobolan S
Methyldienolone (17alpha-methyl-17beta-hydroxyestr-4,9(10)-dien-3-one)	4000	N	
Methyltestosterone (17alpha-methyl-17betahydroxyandrost-4-en-3-one)	4000	N	Android, Oreton, Testred, Virilon
Methyltrienolone (17alpha-methyl-17beta-hydroxyestr-4,9,11-trien-3-one)	4000	N	Metribolone
Methyprylon	2575	N	Noludar
Mibolerone (7alpha,17alpha-dimethyl-17betahydroxyestr-4-en-3-one)	4000	N	Cheque, Matenon
Morphine combination product/50 mg/100 ml or gm	9810	Y	
Nalorphine	9400	Y	Nalline
Nandrolone (17beta-hydroxyestr-4-en-3-one)	4000	N	Deca-Durabolin, Durabolin, Durabolin-50
Norbolethone (13beta,17alpha-diethyl-17betahydroxygon-4-en-3-one)	4000	N	Genabol
Norclostebol (4-chloro-17beta-hydroxyestr-4-en-3-one)	4000	N	Anabol-4-19, Lentabol
Norethandrolone (17alpha-ethyl-17beta-hydroxyestr-4-en-3-one)	4000	N	Nilevar, Pronabol, Solevar
Normethandrolone (17alpha-methyl-17betahydroxyestr-4-en-3-one)	4000	N	Lutenin, Matronal, Orgasteron
Opium combination product 25 mg/du	9809	Y	Paregoric, other combination products
Oxandrolone (17alpha-methyl-17beta-hydroxy-2-oxa-5alpha-androstan-3-one)	4000	N	Anavar, Lonavar, Oxandrin, Provitar, Vasorome
Oxymesterone (17alpha-methyl-4,17betadihydroxyandrost-4-en-3-one)	4000	N	Anamidol, Balnimax, Oranabol, Oranabol 10
Oxymetholone (17alpha-methyl-2-hydroxymethylene-17beta-hydroxy-5alpha-androstan-3-one)	4000	N	Anadrol-50, Adroyd, Anapolon, Anasteron, Pardroyd
Pentobarbital & noncontrolled active ingred.	2271	N	FP-3
Pentobarbital suppository dosage form	2271	N	WANS
Phendimetrazine	1615	N	Plegine, Prelu-2, Bontril, Melfiat, Statobex
Secobarbital & noncontrolled active ingred	2316	N	
Secobarbital suppository dosage form	2316	N	
Stanozolol (17alpha-methyl-17beta-hydroxy-5alphaandrost-2-eno[3,2-c]-pyrazole)	4000	N	N Winstrol, Winstrol-V
Stenbolone (17beta-hydroxy-2-methyl-5alpha-androst-1-en-3-one)	4000	N	
Stimulant compounds previously excepted	1405	N	Mediatric
Sulfondiethylmethane	2600	N	
Sulfonethylmethane	2605	N	
Sulfonmethane	2610	N	
Talbutal	2100	N	Lotusate
Testolactone (13-hydroxy-3-oxo-13,17-secoandrosta-1,4-dien-17-oic acid lactone)	4000	N	Teolit, Teslac

SCHEDULE III

SUBSTANCE	DEA NUMBER	NARCOTIC	OTHER NAMES
Testosterone (17beta-hydroxyandrost-4-en-3-one)	4000	N	Android-T, Androlan, Depotest, Delatestryl
Tetrahydrogestrinone (13beta,17alpha-diethyl-17betahydroxygon-4,9,11-trien-3-one)	4000	N	THG
Thiamylal	2100	N	Surital
Thiopental	2100	N	Pentothal
Tiletamine & Zolazepam Combination Product	7295		Telazol
Trenbolone (17beta-hydroxyestr-4,9,11-trien-3-one)	4000	N	Finaplix-S, Finajet, Parabolan
Vinbarbital	2100	N	Delvinal, vinbarbitone

SCHEDULE IV

SUBSTANCE	DEA NUMBER	NARCOTIC	OTHER NAMES
Alprazolam	2882	N	Xanax
Barbital	2145	N	Veronal, Plexonal, barbitone
Bromazepam	2748	N	Lexotan, Lexatin, Lexotanil
Butorphanol	9720	N	Stadol, Stadol NS, Torbugesic, Torbutrol
Camazepam	2749	N	Albego, Limpidon, Paxor
Cathine	1230	N	Constituent of "Khat" plant, (+)-norpseudoephedrine
Chloral betaine	2460	N	Beta Chlor
Chloral hydrate	2465	N	Noctec
Chlordiazepoxide	2744	N	Librium, Libritabs, Limbitrol, SK-Lygen
Clobazam	2751	N	Urbadan, Urbanyl
Clonazepam	2737	N	Klonopin, Clonopin
Clorazepate	2768	N	Tranxene
Clotiazepam	2752	N	Trecalmo, Rize, Clozan, Veratran
Cloxazolam	2753	N	Akton, Lubalix, Olcadil, Sepazon
Delorazepam	2754	N	
Dexfenfluramine	1670	N	Redux
Dextropropoxyphene dosage forms	9278	Y	Darvon, propoxyphene, Darvocet, Propacet
Diazepam	2765	N	Valium, Diastat
Dichloralphenazone	2467	N	Midrin, dichloralantipyrine
Diethylpropion	1610	N	Tenuate, Tepanil
Difenoxin 1 mg/25 ug AtSO4/du	9167	Y	Motofen
Estazolam	2756	N	ProSom, Domnamid, Eurodin, Nuctalon
Ethchlorvynol	2540	N	Placidyl
Ethinamate	2545	N	Valmid, Valamin
Ethyl loflazepate	2758	N	
Fencamfamin	1760	N	Reactivan
Fenfluramine	1670	N	Pondimin, Ponderal
Fenproporex	1575	N	Gacilin, Solvolip
Fludiazepam	2759	N	

SCHEDULE IV

SUBSTANCE	DEA NUMBER	NARCOTIC	OTHER NAMES
Flunitrazepam	2763	N	Rohypnol, Narcozep, Darkene, Roipnol
Flurazepam	2767	N	Dalmane
Fospropofol	2138	N	Lusedra
Halazepam	2762	N	Paxipam
Haloxazolam	2771	N	
Ketazolam	2772	N	Anxon, Loftran, Solatran, Contamex
Loprazolam	2773	N	
Lorazepam	2885	N	Ativan
Lormetazepam	2774	N	Noctamid
Mazindol	1605	N	Sanorex, Mazanor
Mebutamate	2800	N	Capla
Medazepam	2836	N	Nobrium
Mefenorex	1580	N	Anorexic, Amexate, Doracil, Pondinil
Meprobamate	2820	N	Miltown, Equanil, Deprol, Equagesic, Meprospan
Methohexital	2264	N	Brevital
Methylphenobarbital (mephobarbital)	2250	N	Mebaral, mephobarbital
Midazolam	2884	N	Versed
Modafinil	1680	N	Provigil
Nimetazepam	2837	N	Erimin
Nitrazepam	2834	N	Mogadon
Nordiazepam	2838	N	Nordazepam, Demadar, Madar
Oxazepam	2835	N	Serax, Serenid-D
Oxazolam	2839	N	Serenal, Convertal
Paraldehyde	2585	N	Paral
Pemoline	1530	N	Cylert
Pentazocine	9709	N	Talwin, Talwin NX, Talacen, Talwin Compound
Petrichloral	2591	N	Pentaerythritol chloral, Periclor
Phenobarbital	2285	N	Luminal, Donnatal, Bellergal-S
Phentermine	1640	N	Ionamin, Fastin, Adipex-P, Obe-Nix, Zantryl
Pinazepam	2883	N	Domar
Pipradrol	1750	N	Detaril, Stimolag Fortis
Prazepam	2764	N	Centrax
Quazepam	2881	N	Doral
Sibutramine	1675	N	Meridia
SPA	1635	N	1-dimethylamino-1,2-diphenylethane, Lefetamine
Temazepam	2925	N	Restoril
Tetrazepam	2886	N	Myolastan, Musaril
Triazolam	2887	N	Halcion
Zaleplon	2781	N	Sonata
Zolpidem	2783	N	Ambien, Ivadal, Stilnoct, Stilnox

SCHEDULE V

SUBSTANCE	DEA NUMBER	NARCOTIC	OTHER NAMES
Codeine preparations - 200 mg/100 ml or 100 gm		Y	Cosanyl, Robitussin AC, Cheracol, Cerose, Pediacof
Difenoxin preparations - 0.5 mg/25 ug AtSO4/du		Y	Motofen
Dihydrocodeine preparations 10 mg/100 ml or 100 gm		Y	Cophene-S, various others
Diphenoxylate preparations 2.5 mg/25 ug AtSO4		Y	Lomotil, Logen
Ethylmorphine preparations 100 mg/100 ml or 100 gm		Y	
Lacosamide	2746	N	Vimpat
Opium preparations - 100 mg/100 ml or gm		Y	Parepectolin, Kapectolin PG, Kaolin Pectin P.G.
Pregabalin	2782	N	Lyrica
Pyrovalerone	1485	N	Centroton, Thymergix

FEDERAL TRAFFICKING PENALTIES

DRUG/SCHEDULE	QUANTITY	PENALTIES	QUANTITY	PENALTIES
Cocaine (Schedule II)	500 - 4999 gms mixture	**First Offense:** Not less than 5 yrs, and not more than 40 yrs. If death or serious injury, not less than 20 or more than life. Fine of not more than $5 million if an individual, $25 million if not an individual. **Second Offense:** Not less than 10 yrs, and not more than life. If death or serious injury, life imprisonment. Fine of not more than $8 million if an individual, $50 million if not an individual.	5 kgs or more mixture	**First Offense:** Not less than 10 yrs, and not more than life. If death or serious injury, not less than 20 or more than life. Fine of not more than $10 million if an individual, $50 million if not an individual. **Second Offense:** Not less than 20 yrs, and not more than life. If death or serious injury, life imprisonment. Fine of not more than $20 million if an individual, $75 million if not an individual. **2 or More Prior Offenses:** Life imprisonment.
Cocaine Base (Schedule II)	28-279 gms mixture		280 gms or more mixture	
Fentanyl (Schedule II)	40 - 399 gms mixture		400 gms or more mixture	
Fentanyl Analogue (Schedule I)	10 - 99 gms mixture		100 gms or more mixture	
Heroin (Schedule I)	100 - 999 gms mixture		1 kg or more mixture	
LSD (Schedule I)	1 - 9 gms mixture		10 gms or more mixture	
Methamphetamine (Schedule II)	5 - 49 gms pure or 50 - 499 gms mixture		50 gms or more pure or 500 gms or more mixture	
PCP (Schedule II)	10 - 99 gms pure or 100 - 999 gms mixture		100 gm or more pure or 1 kg or more mixture	

		PENALTIES
Other Schedule I & II drugs (and any drug product containing Gamma Hydroxybutyric Acid)	Any amount	**First Offense:** Not more that 20 yrs. If death or serious injury, not less than 20 yrs, or more than life. Fine $1 million if an individual, $5 million if not an individual. **Second Offense:** Not more than 30 yrs. If death or serious injury, not more than 15 yrs. Fine $2 million if an individual, $10 million if not an individual.
Other Schedule III drugs	Any amount	**First Offense:** Not more than 10 years. If death or serious injury, not more that 15 yrs. Fine not more than $500,000 if an individual, $2.5 million if not an individual. **Second Offense:** Not more than 20 yrs. If death or serious injury, not more than 30 yrs. Fine not more than $1.5 million if an individual, $5 million if not an individual.
All other Schedule IV drugs	Any amount	**First Offense:** Not more than 5 years. Fine not more than $250,000 if an individual, $1 million if not an individual. **Second Offense:** Not more than 10 yrs. Fine not more than $500,000 if an individual, $2 million if not an individual.
Flunitrazepam (Schedule IV)	Less than 1 gm	
All Schedule V drugs	Any amount	**First Offense:** Not more than 1 yr. Fine not more than $100,000 if an individual, $250,000 if not an individual. **Second Offense:** Not more than 4 yrs. Fine not more than $200,000 if an individual, $500,000 if not an individual.

FEDERAL TRAFFICKING PENALTIES — MARIJUANA

DRUG	QUANTITY	1st OFFENSE	2nd OFFENSE *
Marijuana (Schedule I)	1,000 kg or more mixture; or 1,000 or more plants	• Not less than 10 years, not more than life • If death or serious injury, not less than 20 years, not more than life • Fine not more than $4 million if an individual, $10 million if other than an individual	• Not less than 20 years, not more than life • If death or serious injury, mandatory life • Fine not more than $8 million if an individual, $20 million if other than an individual
Marijuana (Schedule I)	100 kg to 999 kg mixture; or 100 to 999 plants	• Not less than 5 years, not more than 40 years • If death or serious injury, not less than 20 years, not more than life • Fine not more than $2 million if an individual, $5 million if other than an individual	• Not less than 10 years, not more than life • If death or serious injury, mandatory life • Fine not more than $4 million if an individual, $10 million if other than an individual
Marijuana (Schedule I)	More than 10 kgs hashish; 50 to 99 kg mixture More than 1 kg of hashish oil; 50 to 99 plants	• Not more than 20 years • If death or serious injury, not less than 20 years, not more than life • Fine $1 million if an individual, $5 million if other than an individual	• Not more than 30 years • If death or serious injury, mandatory life • Fine $2 million if an individual, $10 million if other than individual
Marijuana (Schedule I)	1 to 49 plants; less than 50 kg	• Not more than 5 years • Fine not more than $250,000, $1 million other than individual	• Not more than 10 years • Fine $500,000 if an individual, $2 million if other than individual
Hashish (Schedule I)	10 kg or less		
Hashish Oil (Schedule I)	1 kg or less		

*The minimum sentence for a violation after two or more prior convictions for a felony drug offense have become final is a mandatory term of life imprisonment without release and a fine up to $8 million if an individual and $20 million if other than an individual.

III. U.S. Chemical Control

The Drug Enforcement Administration (DEA) employs a multi-faceted approach to combat drug trafficking which includes enforcement, interdiction, and education. A lesser known approach which combines elements from all three of these facets is chemical control. Large quantities of chemicals are required to synthesize, extract, and purify most illicit drugs. The DEA has long recognized the need to monitor these chemicals as part of its overall drug control strategy.

During the 1980's there was a tremendous increase in the clandestine production of controlled substances, particularly methamphetamine. There was also a proliferation of clandestine laboratories producing controlled substance analogues, very potent and dangerous variations of controlled narcotics, stimulants, and hallucinogens. Furthermore, DEA learned that U.S. firms were exporting large quantities of chemicals, such as acetone, methylethylketone, and potassium permanganate to cocaine producing countries. Significant amounts of these chemicals ultimately were diverted to clandestine cocaine laboratories. It became clear that mandatory controls were needed to control the distribution of these chemicals in order to have an impact on the clandestine laboratory problem.

DEA embarked upon a broad chemical control program in 1989 that began with the Chemical Diversion and Trafficking Act (CDTA) of 1988. The CDTA regulated 12 precursor chemicals, eight essential chemicals, tableting machines and encapsulating machines by imposing recordkeeping and import/export reporting requirements on transactions involving these products. It resulted in effectively reducing the supply of illicit methamphetamine. The number of clandestine laboratories seized in the first three years following the law's implementation reversed the trend of the previous three decades and resulted in a decline. Currently, DEA monitors 41 chemicals which are commonly used in illicit drug production. Maintaining this success requires continuous effort to thwart traffickers' never-ending search for new methods of diversion and new precursor materials.

The foundation of the government's program to prevent chemical diversion is based on additional laws such as the Domestic Chemical Diversion Control Act of 1993 (DCDCA), the Comprehensive Methamphetamine Control Act of 1996 (MCA), the Methamphetamine Anti-Proliferation Act of 2000 (MAPA), and the Combat Methamphetamine Epidemic Act of 2005 (CMEA). This is illustrated by changes in the patterns of diversion:

» When the quantity of U.S. chemicals shipped to cocaine manufacturing areas declined, chemical suppliers from other parts of the world emerged as new sources of supply. The U.S. government then undertook an aggressive international campaign to educate and elicit the support of other nations in establishing chemical controls. Today, there is a broad level of international agreement regarding the actions that must be taken to achieve chemical control. Many nations have passed laws to prevent the diversion of chemicals.

» As a result of government controls, ephedrine and other chemicals used to manufacture methamphetamine became more difficult to divert. Traffickers then began using over-the-counter capsules and tablets that contained these ingredients. As chemicals rendered into legitimate medicines purportedly for the commercial market, these products were exempted from the CDTA requirements. The DCDCA closed this loophole and required DEA registration for all manufacturers, distributors, importers, and exporters of List I chemicals. It also established recordkeeping and reporting requirements for transactions in single-entity ephedrine products.

» When single-entity ephedrine products became regulated, drug traffickers turned to pseudoephedrine. This was addressed by the MCA which expanded regulatory control of lawfully marketed drug products containing ephedrine, pseudoephedrine, and phenylpropanolamine (PPA)[1].

» MAPA focused on the continuing reta l level diversion by constricting retail transactions of pseudoephedrine and PPA drug products. It reduced the threshold for such transactions from 24 grams to nine grams of pseudoephedrine or PPA base in a single transaction and limited package sizes to contain no more than three grams of pseudoephedrine or PPA base. The Act also increased penalties for chemical diversion and provided for restitution to the government for cleanup costs.

» The CMEA further restricted retail level transactions by redefining nonprescription products that contain ephedrine, pseudoephedrine, and PPA as "scheduled listed chemical products (SLCPs)." The Act requires all regulated sellers of SLCPs to complete a required training and self-certification process effective September 30, 2006. On this date, stores were required to keep all SLCPs behind the counter or in a locked cabinet. Consumers wishing to purchase SLCPs are required to show identification and sign a logbook for each purchase. The Act also implements daily sales limits of 3.6 grams per purchaser and purchase limits of nine grams of these products in a 30 day period to any person.

All of these Federal laws (CDTA, DCDCA, MCA, MAPA, and CMEA) imposed varying degrees of reporting requirements on the chemical and pharmaceutical industries. Yet the involvement of private industry and the public should not be limited to the laws enacted by Congress. The voluntary support by industry constitutes a powerful resource for protecting the health and safety of the nation. DEA encourages each firm to be vigilant and to become a partner in combating the diversion of chemicals used in illegal drug production.

It is DEA's goal to effectively regulate while maintaining a positive working relationship with the regulated community and seeks to educate the regulated community on the various laws regarding precursor chemicals and their implementing regulations. DEA understands that it can best serve the public interest by working in voluntary cooperation with the chemical industry in developing programs designed to prevent the diversion of regulated chemicals into the illicit market.

---

[1] *Due to concerns regarding harmful side effects that phenylpropanolamine (PPA) can have, on November 6, 2000 the Food and Drug Administration invoked a voluntary withdrawal of over-the counter PPA products intended for human consumption.*

Listed Chemicals regulated under the Controlled Substances Act

See 21, C.F.R. §§ 1309, 1310, and 1314 for details

August 14, 2007

CONTROLLED SUBSTANCE PRODUCED

LIST I	Amphetamine	Cocaine	N,N-Dimethylamphetamine	Ethylamphetamine	Fentanyl & Analogues	GHB	Heroin	LSD	MDA	MDE	MDMA	Methamphetamine	Methaqualone	Methcathinone	4-Methylaminorex	Phencyclidine (PCP)	Phenyl-2-Propanone	THRESHOLDS DOMESTIC	IMPORTS & EXPORTS
																		KILOGRAMS	
1. N-Acetylanthranilic Acid [2]													▲					40	40
2. Anthranilic Acid [2]													▲					30	30
3. Benzaldehyde	▲															▲		4	4
4. Benzyl Cyanide																▲		1	1
5. Ephedrine												▲		▲				0	0
6. Ergonovine								▲										0.010	0.010
7. Ergotamine								▲										0.020	0.020
8. Ethylamine [1]				▲						▲								1	1
9. Gamma-Butyrolactone (GBL)						▲												0	0
10. Hydriodic Acid												■						1.7	1.7
11. Hypophosphorous Acid [1]	■											■						0	0
12. Iodine	■											■						0	0
13. Isosafrole									▲	▲	▲							4	4
14. Methylamine [1]										▲	▲							1	1
15. 3, 4-Methylenedioxyphenyl-2-Propanone									▲	▲	▲							4	4
16. N-Methylephedrine [3]			▲															1	1
17. N-Methylpseudoephedrine [3]			▲															1	1
18. N-phenethyl-4-Piperidone (NPP)					▲													0	0
19. Nitroethane	▲								▲								▲	2.5	2.5
20. Norpseudoephedrine [3]	▲														▲			2.5	2.5
21. Phenylacetic Acid [2]																	▲	1	1
22. Phenylpropanolamine [3&7]	▲														▲			2.5	2.5
23. Phosphorus (red)	■											■						0	0
24. Phosphorus (white or yellow)	■											■						0	0
25. Piperidine [1]																▲		0.500	0.500
26. Piperonal									▲	▲	▲							4	4
27. Propionic Anhydride					▲													0.001	0.001
28. Pseudoephedrine [3&7]												▲		▲				1	1
29. Safrole									▲	▲	▲							4	4

Listed Chemicals regulated under the Controlled Substances Act

See 21, C.F.R. §§ 1309, 1310, and 1314 for details

August 14, 2007

CONTROLLED SUBSTANCE PRODUCED

	Amphetamine	Cocaine	N,N-Dimethylamphetamine	Ethylamphetamine	Fentanyl & Analogues	GHB	Heroin	LSD	MDA	MDE	MDMA	Methamphetamine	Methaqualone	Methcathinone	4-Methylaminorex	Phencyclidine (PCP)	Phenyl-2-Propanone	THRESHOLDS Domestic	THRESHOLDS Imports & Exports
30. Acetic Anhydride						▲						▲					▲	1,023	1,023
31. Acetone		●					●	●	●	●	●	●						150	1,500
32. Benzyl Chloride											▲							1	4
33. Ethyl Ether	●	●		●			●	●	●	●	●	●	●			●	●	135.8	1,364
34. Hydrochloric Acid [5&6]	■	■	■	■	■		■	■	■	■	■	■	■	■		■		N/C	222.3
34a. Hydrogen Chloride Gas [5&6]	■	■	■	■	■		■	■	■	■	■	■	■	■		■		0	27
35. Methyl Ethyl Ketone (2-Butanone)		●					●	●	●	●	●							145	1,455
36. Methyl Isobutyl Ketone [4]		●					●		●	●	●							N/C	1,523
37. Potassium Permanganate		■																55	500
38. Sodium Permanganate		■																55	500
39. Sulfuric Acid [5&6]	■	■							■	■	■	■				■		N/C	347
40. Toluene		●			●							●				●	●	159	1,591

DOMESTIC — IMPORTS & EXPORTS — KILOGRAMS

KEY

● = Solvent   ■ = Reagent   ▲ = Precursor

---

[1] and its salts
[2] and its salts and esters
[3] and its salts, optical isomers, and salts of optical isomers
[4] Exports only to all Western Hemisphere except Canada
[5] Exports to all South American countries & Panama — Domestic for HCl gas
[6] Threshold for HCl acid and sulfuric acid is 50 gallons, the equivalent weight in kilograms is shown
[7] For pseudoephedrine, phenylpropanolamine and ephedrine drug products, see 21 USC § 802 (45)(A) and 21 CFR Part 1314
  N/C – Not Controlled

IV. Introduction to Drug Classes

The Controlled Substances Act (CSA) regulates five classes of drugs:

→ Narcotics

→ Depressants

→ Stimulants

→ Hallucinogens

→ Anabolic steroids

Each class has distinguishing properties, and drugs within each class often produce similar effects. However, all controlled substances, regardless of class, share a number of common features. This introduction will familiarize you with these shared features and define the terms frequently associated with these drugs.

All controlled substances have abuse potential or are immediate precursors to substances with abuse potential. With the exception of anabolic steroids, controlled substances are abused to alter mood, thought, and feeling through their actions on the central nervous system (brain and spinal cord). Some of these drugs alleviate pain, anxiety, or depression. Some induce sleep and others energize.

Though some controlled substances are therapeutically useful, the "feel good" effects of these drugs contribute to their abuse. The extent to which a substance is reliably capable of producing intensely pleasurable feelings (euphoria) increases the likel hood of that substance being abused.

DRUG ABUSE

When drugs are used in a manner or amount inconsistent with the medical or social patterns of a culture, it is called drug abuse. The non-sanctioned use of substances controlled in Schedules I through V of the CSA is considered drug abuse. While legal pharmaceuticals placed under control in the CSA are prescribed and used by patients for medical treatment, the use of these same pharmaceuticals outside the scope of sound medical practice is drug abuse.

DEPENDENCE

In addition to having abuse potential, most controlled substances are capable of producing dependence, either physical or psychological.

Physical Dependence

Physical dependence refers to the changes that have occurred in the body after repeated use of a drug that necessitates the continued administration of the drug to prevent a withdrawal syndrome. This withdrawal syndrome can range from mildly unpleasant to life-threatening and is dependent on a number of factors, such as:

→ The drug being used

→ The dose and route of administration

→ Concurrent use of other drugs

→ Frequency and duration of drug use

→ The age, sex, health, and genetic makeup of the user

Psychological Dependence

Psychological dependence refers to the perceived "need" or "craving" for a drug. Individuals who are psychologically dependent on a particular substance often feel that they cannot function without continued use of that substance. While physical dependence disappears within days or weeks after drug use stops, psychological dependence can last much longer and is one of the primary reasons for relapse (initiation of drug use after a period of abstinence).

Contrary to common belief, physical dependence is not addiction. Wh le addicts are usually physically dependent on the drug they are abusing, physical dependence can exist without addiction. For example, patients who take narcotics for chronic pain management or benzodiazepines to treat anxiety are likely to be physically dependent on that medication.

ADDICTION

Addiction is defined as compulsive drug-seeking behavior where acquiring and using a drug becomes the most important activity in the user's life. This definition implies a loss of control regarding drug use, and the addict will continue to use a drug despite serious medical and/or social consequences. In 2009, an estimated 21.8 million Americans aged 12 or older were current (past month) illicit drug users, meaning they had used an illicit drug during the month prior to the survey interview. This estimate represents 8.7 percent of the population aged 12 or older. Illicit drugs include marijuana/hashish, cocaine (including crack), heroin, hallucinogens, inhalants, or prescription-type psychotherapeutics used nonmedically. [1]

Drugs within a class are often compared with each other with terms like potency and efficacy. Potency refers to the amount of a drug that must be taken to produce a certain effect, while efficacy refers to whether or not a drug is capable of producing a given effect regardless of dose. Both the strength and the ability of a substance to produce certain effects play a role in whether that drug is selected by the drug abuser.

It is important to keep in mind that the effects produced by any drug can vary significantly and is largely dependent on the dose and route of administration. Concurrent use of other drugs can enhance or block an effect, and substance abusers often take more than one drug to boost the desired effects or counter unwanted side effects. The risks associated with drug abuse cannot be accurately predicted because each user has his/her own unique sensitivity to a drug. There are a number of theories that attempt to explain these differences, and it is clear that a genetic component may predispose an individual to certain toxicities or even addictive behavior.

Youth are especially vulnerable to drug abuse. According to NIDA, young Americans engaged in extraordinary levels of illicit drug use in the last third of the twentieth century. Today, about 47% of young people have used an illicit drug by the time they leave high school and about 16 percent of eighth, tenth, and twelfth graders are current (within the past month) users. [2]

The behaviors associated with teen and preteen drug use often result in tragic consequences with untold harm to others, themselves, and their families. For example, an analysis of data from the National Survey on Drug Use and Health indicates that youth between the ages of 12 and 17 who had engaged in fighting or other delinquent behaviors were more likely than other youths to have used illicit drugs in the past month. For example, in 2009, past-month illicit drug use was reported by 18.8 percent of youths who had gotten into a serious fight at school or work in the past year, compared with 7.7 percent of those who had not engaged in fighting, and by 38.3 percent of those who had stolen or tried to steal something worth over $50 in the past year compared with 8.7 percent of those who had not attempted or engaged in such theft. [3]

In the sections that follow, each of the five classes of drugs is reviewed and various drugs within each class are profiled. Although marijuana is classified in the CSA as a hallucinogen, a separate section is dedicated to that topic. There are also a number of substances that are abused but not regulated under the CSA. Alcohol and tobacco, for example, are specifically exempt from control by the CSA. In addition, a whole group of substances called inhalants are commonly available and widely abused by children. Control of these substances under the CSA would not only impede legitimate commerce, but also would likely have little effect on the abuse of these substances by youngsters. An energetic campaign aimed at educating both adults and youth about inhalants is more likely to prevent their abuse. To that end, a section is dedicated to providing information on inhalants.

---

[1] Results from the 2009 National Survey on Drug Use and Health: Volume I. Summary of National Findings, U.S. Department of Health and Human Services, Substance Abuse and Mental Health Services Administration

[2] Monitoring the Future Survey, 2009; National Institute on Drug Abuse, National Institutes of Health, U.S. Department of Health and Human Services

[3] National Survey on Drug Use and Health, 2009; U.S. Department of Health and Human Services, Substance Abuse and Mental Health Services Administration

V. Narcotics

WHAT ARE NARCOTICS?

Also known as "opioids," the term "narcotic" comes from the Greek word for "stupor" and originally referred to a variety of substances that dulled the senses and relieved pain. Though some people still refer to all drugs as "narcotics," today "narcotic" refers to opium, opium derivatives, and their semi-synthetic substitutes. A more current term for these drugs, with less uncertainty regarding its meaning, is "opioid." Examples include the illicit drug heroin and pharmaceutical drugs like OxyContin®, Vicodin®, codeine, morphine, methadone, and fentanyl.

WHAT IS THEIR ORIGIN?

The poppy papaver somniferum is the source for all natural opioids, whereas synthetic opioids are made entirely in a lab and include meperidine, fentanyl, and methadone. Semi-synthetic opioids are synthesized from naturally occurring opium products, such as morphine and codeine, and include heroin, oxycodone, hydrocodone, and hydromorphone. Teens can obtain narcotics from friends, family members, medicine cabinets, pharmacies, nursing homes, hospitals, hospices, doctors, and the Internet.

OxyContin® 160 mg tablet

Heroin

What are common street names?
Street names for various narcotics/opioids include:

→ Smack, Horse, Mud, Brown Sugar, Junk, Black Tat, Big H, Paregoric, Dover's Powder, MPTP (New Heroin), Hilbilly Heroin, Lean or Purple Drank, OC, Ox, Oxy, Oxycotton, Sippin Syrup

What do they look like?
Narcotics/opioids come in various forms, including:

→ Tablets, capsules, skin patches, powder, chunks in varying colors (from white to shades of brown and black), liquid form for oral use and injection, syrups, suppositories, and lollipops

How are they abused?
→ Narcotics/opioids can be swallowed, smoked, sniffed, or injected.

What is their effect on the mind?

Besides their medical use, narcotics/opioids produce a general sense of well-being by reducing tension, anxiety, and aggression. These effects are helpful in a therapeutic setting but contribute to the drugs' abuse. Narcotic/opioid use comes with a variety of unwanted effects, including drowsiness, inability to concentrate, and apathy.

Psychological dependence

Use can create psychological dependence. Long after the physical need for the drug has passed, the addict may continue to think and talk about using drugs and feel overwhelmed coping with daily activities. Relapse is common if there are not changes to the physical environment or the behavioral motivators that prompted the abuse in the first place.

What is their effect on the body?

Narcotics/opioids are prescribed by doctors to treat pain, suppress cough, cure diarrhea, and put people to sleep. Effects depend heavily on the dose, how it's taken, and previous exposure to the drug. Negative effects include:

→ Slowed physical activity, constriction of the pupils, flushing of the face and neck, constipation, nausea, vomiting, and slowed breathing

As the dose is increased, both the pain relief and the harmful effects become more pronounced. Some of these preparations are so potent that a single dose can be lethal to an inexperienced user. However, except in cases of extreme intoxication, there is no loss of motor coordination or slurred speech.

Physical dependence and withdrawal

Physical dependence is a consequence of chronic opioid use, and withdrawal takes place when drug use is discontinued. The intensity and character of the physical symptoms experienced during withdrawal are directly related to the particular drug used, the total daily dose, the interval between doses, the duration of use and the health and personality of the user. These symptoms usually appear shortly before the time of the next scheduled dose.

Early withdrawal symptoms often include:

→ Watery eyes, runny nose, yawning, and sweating

As the withdrawal worsens, symptoms can include:

→ Restlessness, irritability, loss of appetite, nausea, tremors, drug craving, severe depression, vomiting, increased heart rate and blood pressure, and chills alternating with flushing and excessive sweating

However, without intervention, the withdrawal usually runs its course, and most physical symptoms disappear within days or weeks, depending on the particular drug.

What are their overdose effects?

Overdoses of narcotics are not uncommon and can be fatal. Physical signs of narcotics/opioid overdose include:

→ Constricted (pinpoint) pupils, cold clammy skin, confusion, convulsions, extreme drowsiness, and slowed breathing

Which drugs cause similar effects?

With the exception of pain relief and cough suppression, most central nervous system depressants (like barbiturates, benzodiazepines, and alcohol) have similar effects, including slowed breathing, tolerance, and dependence.

What is their legal status in the United States?

Narcotics/opioids are controlled substances that vary from Schedule I to Schedule V, depending on their medical usefulness, abuse potential, safety, and drug dependence profile. Schedule I narcotics, like heroin, have no medical use in the U.S. and are illegal to distrbute, purchase, or use outside of medical research.

Heroin

WHAT IS HEROIN?

Heroin is a highly addictive drug and the most rapidly acting of the opiates.

WHAT IS ITS ORIGIN?

Heroin is processed from morphine, a naturally occurring substance extracted from the seed pod of certain varieties of poppy plants grown in:

→ Southeast Asia (Thailand, Laos, and Myanmar (Burma)), Southwest Asia (Afghanistan and Pakistan), Mexico, and Colombia

It comes in several forms, the main one being "black tar" from Mexico (found primarily in the western United States) and white heroin from Colombia (primarily sold on the East Coast).

Heroin

What are common street names?

Common street names for heroin include:

→ Big H, Black Tar, Chiva, Hell Dust, Horse, Negra, Smack, and Thunder

What does it look like?

Heroin is typically sold as a white or brownish powder, or as the black sticky substance known on the streets as "black tar heroin." Although purer heroin is becoming more common, most street heroin is "cut" with other drugs or with substances such as sugar, starch, powdered milk, or quinine.

How is it abused?

Heroin can be injected, smoked, or sniffed/snorted. High purity heroin is usually snorted or smoked.

What is its effect on the mind?

Because it enters the brain so rapidly, heroin is particularly addictive, both psychologically and physically. Heroin abusers report feeling a surge of euphoria or "rush," followed by a twilight state of sleep and wakefulness.

What is its effect on the body?

One of the most significant effects of heroin use is addiction. With regular heroin use, tolerance to the drug develops. Once this happens, the abuser must use more heroin to achieve the same intensity. As higher doses of the drug are used over time, physical dependence and addiction to the drug develop.

Physical symptoms of heroin use include:

→ Drowsiness, respiratory depression, constricted pupils, nausea, a warm flushing of the skin, dry mouth, and heavy extremities

What are its overdose effects?

Because heroin abusers do not know the actual strength of the drug or its true contents, they are at a high risk of overdose or death.

The effects of a heroin overdose are:

→ Slow and shallow breathing, blue lips and fingernails, clammy skin, convulsions, coma, and possible death

Which drugs cause similar effects?

Other opioids such as OxyContin®, Vicodin®, codeine, morphine, methadone, and fentanyl can cause similar effects as heroin.

What is its legal status in the United States?

Heroin is a Schedule I substance under the Controlled Substances Act meaning that it has a high potential for abuse, no currently accepted medical use in treatment in the United States, and a lack of accepted safety for use under medical supervision.

Hydromorphone

WHAT IS HYDROMORPHONE?

Hydromorphone belongs to a class of drugs called "opioids," which includes morphine. It has an analgesic potency of two to eight times that of morphine, but has a shorter duration of action and greater sedative properties.

WHAT IS ITS ORIGIN?

Hydromorphone is legally manufactured and distributed in the United States. However, abusers can obtain hydromorphone from forged prescriptions, "doctor-shopping," theft from pharmacies, and from friends and acquaintances.

What are the street names?
Common street names include:

→ D, Dillies, Dust, Footballs, Juice, and Smack

What does it look like?
Hydromorphone comes in:

→ Tablets, rectal suppositories, oral solutions, and injectable formulations

How is it abused?
Users may abuse hydromorphone tablets by ingesting them. Injectable solutions, as well as tablets that have been crushed and dissolved in a solution may be injected as a substitute for heroin.

What is its effect on the mind?
When used as a drug of abuse, and not under a doctor's supervision, hydromorphone is taken to produce feelings of euphoria, relaxation, sedation, and reduced anxiety. It may also cause mental clouding, changes in mood, nervousness, and restlessness. It works centrally (in the brain) to reduce pain and suppress cough. Hydromorphone use is associated with both physiological and psychological dependence.

What is its effect on the body?
Hydromorphone may cause:

→ Constipation, pupillary constriction, urinary retention, nausea, vomiting, respiratory depression, dizziness, impaired coordination, loss of appetite, rash, slow or rapid heartbeat, and changes in blood pressure

What are its overdose effects?
Acute overdose of hydromorphone can produce:

→ Severe respiratory depression, drowsiness progressing to stupor or coma, lack of skeletal muscle tone, cold and clammy skin, constricted pupils, and reduction in blood pressure and heart rate

Severe overdose may result in death due to respiratory depression.

Which drugs cause similar effects?
Drugs that have similar effects include:

→ Heroin, morphine, hydrocodone, fentanyl, and oxycodone

What is its legal status in the United States?
Hydromorphone is a Schedule II drug under the Controlled Substances Act with an accepted medical use as a pain reliever. Hydromorphone has a high potential for abuse and use may lead to severe psychological or physical dependence.

Methadone

WHAT IS METHADONE?

Methadone is a synthetic (man-made) narcotic.

WHAT IS ITS ORIGIN?

German scientists synthesized methadone during World War II because of a shortage of morphine. Methadone was introduced into the United States in 1947 as an analgesic (Dolophinel).

What are common street names?

Common street names include:

→ Amidone, Chocolate Chip Cookies, Fizzies, Maria, Pastora, Salvia, Street Methadone, and Wafer

What does it look like?

Methadone is available as a tablet, disc, oral solution, or injectable liquid. Tablets are available in 5 mg and 10 mg formulations. As of January 1, 2008, manufacturers of methadone hydrochloride tablets 40 mg (dispersible) have voluntarily agreed to restrict distribution of this formulation to only those facilities authorized for detoxification and maintenance treatment of opioid addiction, and hospitals. Manufacturers will instruct their wholesale distributors to discontinue supplying this formulation to any facility not meeting the above criteria.

How is it abused?

Methadone can be swallowed or injected.

What is its effect on the mind?

Abuse of methadone can lead to psychological dependence.

What is its effect on the body?

When an individual uses methadone, he/she may experience physical symptoms like sweating, itchy skin, or sleepiness. Individuals who abuse methadone risk becoming tolerant of and physically dependent on the drug.

When use is stopped, individuals may experience withdrawal symptoms including:

→ Anxiety, muscle tremors, nausea, diarrhea, vomiting, and abdominal cramps

What are its overdose effects?

The effects of a methadone overdose are:

→ Slow and shallow breathing, blue fingernails and lips, stomach spasms, clammy skin, convulsions, weak pulse, coma, and possible death

Which drugs cause similar effects?

Although chemically unlike morphine or heroin, methadone produces many of the same effects.

What is its legal status in the United States?

Methadone is a Schedule II drug under the Controlled Substances Act. While it may legally be used under a doctor's supervision, its non-medical use is illegal.

Methadone

Morphine

WHAT IS MORPHINE?

Morphine is a non-synthetic narcotic with a high potential for abuse and is the principal constituent of opium. It is one of the most effective drugs known for the relief of severe pain.

WHAT IS ITS ORIGIN?

In the United States, a small percentage of the morphine obtained from opium is used directly for pharmaceutical products. The remaining morphine is processed into codeine and other derivatives.

What are common street names?

Common street names include:

→ Dreamer, Emsel, First Line, God's Drug, Hows, M.S., Mister Blue, Morf, Morpho, and Unkie

What does it look like?

Morphine is marketed under generic and brand name products, including:

→ MS-Contin®, Oramorph SR®, MSIR®, Roxanol®, Kadian®, and RMS®

How is it abused?

Traditionally, morphine was almost exclusively used by injection, but the variety of pharmaceutical forms that it is marketed as today support its use by oral and other routes of administration.

Forms include:

→ Oral solutions, immediate-and sustained-release tablets and capsules, suppositories, and injectable preparations

Those dependent on morphine prefer injection because the drug enters the blood stream more quickly.

What is its effect on the mind?

Morphine's effects include euphoria and relief of pain. Chronic use of morphine results in tolerance and physical and psychological dependence.

What is its effect on the body?

Morphine use results in relief from physical pain, decrease in hunger, and inhibition of the cough reflex.

What are its overdose effects?

Overdose effects include:

→ Cold, clammy skin, lowered blood pressure, sleepiness, slowed breathing, slow pulse rate, coma, and possible death

Which drugs cause similar effects?

Drugs causing similar effects as morphine include:

→ Opium, codeine, heroin, methadone, hydrocodone, fentanyl, and oxycodone

What is its legal status in the United States?

Morphine is a Schedule II narcotic under the Controlled Substances Act.

Poppy papaver somniferum, the source for all non-synthetic opioids

Opium

WHAT IS OPIUM?

Opium is a highly addictive non-synthetic narcotic that is extracted from the poppy plant, Papaver somniferum. The opium poppy is the key source for many narcotics, including morphine, codeine, and heroin.

WHAT IS ITS ORIGIN?

The poppy plant, Papaver somniferum, is the source of opium. It was grown in the Mediterranean region as early as 5,000 B.C., and has since been cultivated in a number of countries throughout the world. The milky fluid that seeps from its incisions in the unripe seed pod of this poppy has been scraped by hand and air-dried to produce what is known as opium.

A more modern method of harvesting for pharmaceutical use is by the industrial poppy straw process of extracting alkaloids from the mature dried plant (concentrate of poppy straw). All opium and poppy straw used for pharmaceutical products are imported into the United States from legitimate sources in regulated countries.

What are common street names?
Common street names include:

→ Ah-pen-yen, Aunti, Aunti Emma, Big O, Black Pill, Chandoo, Chandu, Chinese Molasses, Chinese Tobacco, Dopium, Dover's Powder, Dream Gun, Dream Stick, Dreams, Easing Powder, Fi-do-nie, Gee, God's Medicine, Gondola, Goric, Great Tobacco, Guma, Hop/hops, Joy Plant, Midnight Oil, Mira, O, O.P., Ope, Pen Yan, Pin Gon, Pox, Skee, Toxy, Toys, When-shee, Ze, and Zero

What does it look like?
Opium can be a liquid, solid, or powder, but most poppy straw concentrate is available commercially as a fine brownish powder.

How is it abused?
Opium can be smoked, intravenously injected, or taken in pill form. Opium is also abused in combination with other drugs. For example, "Black" is a combination of marijuana, opium, and methamphetamine, and "Buddha" is potent marijuana spiked with opium.

What is its effect on the mind?
The intensity of opium's euphoric effects on the brain depends on the dose and route of administration. It works quickly when smoked because the opiate chemicals pass into the lungs, where they are quickly absorbed and then sent to the brain. An opium "high" is very similar to a heroin "high"; users experience a euphoric rush, followed by relaxation and the relief of physical pain.

What is its effect on the body?
Opium inhibits muscle movement in the bowels leading to constipation. It also can dry out the mouth and mucous membranes in the nose. Opium use leads to physical and psychological dependence, and can lead to overdose.

What are its overdose effects?
Overdose effects include:

→ Slow breathing, seizures, dizziness, weakness, loss of consciousness, coma, and possible death

Which drugs cause similar effects?
Drugs that cause similar effects include:

→ Morphine, codeine, heroin, methadone, hydroquinone, fentanyl, and oxycodone

What is its legal status in the United States?
Opium is a Schedule II drug under the Controlled Substances Act. Most opioids are Schedule II, III, IV, or V drugs. Some drugs that are derived from opium, such as heroin, are Schedule I drugs.

Oxycodone

WHAT IS OXYCODONE?

Oxycodone is a semi-synthetic narcotic analgesic and historically has been a popular drug of abuse among the narcotic abusing population.

WHAT IS ITS ORIGIN?

Oxycodone is synthesized from thebaine, a constituent of the poppy plant.

What are common street names?

Common street names for Oxycodone include:

→ Hillbilly Heroin, Kicker, OC, Ox, Roxy, Perc, and Oxy

What does it look like?

Oxycodone is marketed alone as OxyContin® in 10, 20, 40 and 80 mg controlled-release tablets and other immediate-release capsules like 5 mg OxyIR®. It is also marketed in combination products with aspirin such as Percodan® or acetaminophen such as Roxicet®.

How is it abused?

Oxycodone is abused orally or intravenously. The tablets are crushed and sniffed or dissolved in water and injected. Others heat a tablet that has been placed on a piece of foil then inhale the vapors.

What is its effect on the mind?

Euphoria and feelings of relaxation are the most common effects of oxycodone on the brain, which explains its high potential for abuse.

What is its effect on the body?

Physiological effects of oxycodone include:

→ Pain relief, sedation, respiratory depression, constipation, papillary constriction, and cough suppression. Extended or chronic use of oxycodone containing acetaminophen may cause severe liver damage.

What are its overdose effects?

Overdose effects include:

→ Extreme drowsiness, muscle weakness, confusion, cold and clammy skin, pinpoint pupils, shallow breathing, slow heart rate, fainting, coma, and possible death

Which drugs cause similar effects?

Drugs that cause similar effects to Oxycodone include:

→ Opium, codeine, heroin, methadone, hydrocodone, fentanyl, and morphine

What is its legal status in the United States?

Oxycodone products are in Schedule II of the federal Controlled Substances Act of 1970.

VI. Stimulants

WHAT ARE STIMULANTS?

Stimulants speed up the body's systems. This class of drugs includes:

→ Prescription drugs such as amphetamines [Adderall® and Dexedrine®], methylphenidate [Concerta® and Ritalin®], diet aids [such as Didrex®, Bontril®, Preludin®, Fastin®, Adipex P®, Ionomin®, and Meridia®] and illicitly produced drugs such as methamphetamine, cocaine, and methcathinone.

WHAT IS THEIR ORIGIN?

Stimulants are diverted from legitimate channels and clandestinely manufactured exclusively for the illicit market.

Ritalin® SR 20mg tablet

Crack Cocaine

What are common street names?
Common street names include:

→ Bennies, Black Beauties, Cat, Coke, Crank, Crystal, Flake, Ice, Pellets, R-Ball, Skippy, Snow, Speed, Uppers, and Vitamin R

What do they look like?
Stimulants come in the form of:

→ Pills, powder, rocks, and injectable liquids

How are they abused?
Stimulants can be pills or capsules that are swallowed. Smoking, snorting, or injecting stimulants produces a sudden sensation known as a "rush" or a "flash."

Abuse is often associated with a pattern of binge use — sporadically consuming large doses of stimulants over a short period of time. Heavy users may inject themselves every few hours, continuing until they have depleted their drug supply or reached a point of delirium, psychosis, and physical exhaustion. During heavy use, all other interests become secondary to recreating the initial euphoric rush.

What is their effect on the mind?

When used as drugs of abuse and not under a doctor's supervision, stimulants are frequently taken to:

→ Produce a sense of exhilaration, enhance self esteem, improve mental and physical performance, increase activity, reduce appetite, extend wakefulness for prolonged period, and "get high"

Chronic, high-dose use is frequently associated with agitation, hostility, panic, aggression, and suicidal or homicidal tendencies.

Paranoia, sometimes accompanied by both auditory and visual hallucinations, may also occur.

Tolerance, in which more and more drug is needed to produce the usual effects, can develop rapidly, and psychological dependence occurs. In fact, the strongest psychological dependence observed occurs with the more potent stimulants, such as amphetamine, methylphenidate, methamphetamine, cocaine and methcathinone.

Abrupt cessation is commonly followed by depression, anxiety, drug craving, and extreme fatigue, known as a "crash."

What is their effect on the body?

Stimulants are sometimes referred to as uppers and reverse the effects of fatigue on both mental and physical tasks. Therapeutic levels of stimulants can produce exhilaration, extended wakefulness, and loss of appetite. These effects are greatly intensified when large doses of stimulants are taken.

Taking too large a dose at one time or taking large doses over an extended period of time may cause such physical side effects as:

→ Dizziness, tremors, headache, flushed skin, chest pain with palpitations, excessive sweating, vomiting, and abdominal cramps

What are their overdose effects?

In overdose, unless there is medical intervention, high fever, convulsions, and cardiovascular collapse may precede death. Because accidental death is partially due to the effects of stimulants on the body's cardiovascular and temperature-regulating systems, physical exertion increases the hazards of stimulant use.

Which drugs cause similar effects?

Some hallucinogenic substances, such as Ecstasy, have a stimulant component to their activity.

What is their legal status in the United States?

Many stimulants have a legitimate medical use for the treatment of conditions such as obesity, narcolepsy, and attention deficit and hyperactivity disorder. Such stimulants vary in their level of control from Schedules II to IV, depending on their potential for abuse and dependence.

A number of stimulants have no medical use in the United States but have a high potential for abuse. These stimulants are controlled in Schedule I. Some prescription stimulants are not controlled, and some stimulants like tobacco and caffeine don't require a prescription — though society's recognition of their adverse effects has resulted in a proliferation of caffeine-free products and efforts to discourage cigarette smoking.

Stimulant chemicals in over-the-counter products, such as ephedrine and pseudoephedrine can be found in allergy and cold medicine. As required by The Combat Methamphetamine Epidemic Act of 2005, a retail outlet must store these products out of reach of customers, either behind the counter or in a locked cabinet. Regulated sellers are required to maintain a written or electronic form of a logbook to record sales of these products. In order to purchase these products, customers must now show a photo identification issued by a state or federal government. They are also required to write or enter into the logbook: their name, signature, address, date, and time of sale. In addition to the above, there are daily and monthly sales limits set for customers.

Amphetamines

WHAT ARE AMPHETAMINES?

Amphetamines are stimulants that speed up the body's system. Many are legally prescribed and used to treat attention-deficit hyperactivity disorder (ADHD).

WHAT IS THEIR ORIGIN?

Amphetamine was first marketed in the 1930s as Benzedrine® in an over-the-counter inhaler to treat nasal congestion. By 1937 amphetamine was available by prescription in tablet form and was used in the treatment of the sleeping disorder, narcolepsy, and ADHD.

Over the years, the use and abuse of clandestinely produced amphetamines have spread. Today, clandestine laboratory production of amphetamines has mushroomed, and the abuse of the drug has increased dramatically.

What are common street names?
Common street names include:

→ Bennies, Black Beauties, Crank, Ice, Speed, and Uppers

What do they look like?
Amphetamines can look like pills or powder. Common prescription amphetamines include methylphenidate (Ritalin® or Ritalin SR®), amphetamine and dextroamphetamine (Adderall®), and dextroamphetamine (Dexedrine®).

How are they abused?
Amphetamines are generally taken orally or injected. However, the addition of "ice," the slang name of crystallized methamphetamine hydrochloride, has promoted smoking as another mode of administration. Just as "crack" is smokable cocaine, "ice" is smokable methamphetamine.

What is their effect on the mind?
The effects of amphetamines and methamphetamine are similar to cocaine, but their onset is slower and their duration is longer. In contrast to cocaine, which is quickly removed from the brain and is almost completely metabolized, methamphetamine remains in the central nervous system longer, and a larger percentage of the drug remains unchanged in the body, producing prolonged stimulant effects.

Chronic abuse produces a psychosis that resembles schizophrenia and is characterized by: Paranoia, picking at the skin, preoccupation with one's own thoughts, and auditory and visual hallucinations. Violent and erratic behavior is frequently seen among chronic abusers of amphetamines and methamphetamine.

What is their effect on the body?
Physical effects of amphetamine use include:

→ Increased blood pressure and pulse rates, insomnia, loss of appetite, and physical exhaustion

What are their overdose effects?
Overdose effects include:

→ Agitation, increased body temperature, hallucinations, convulsions, and possible death

Which drugs cause similar effects?
Drugs that cause similar effects include:

→ Dexmethylphendiate, phentermine, benzphetamine, phendimetrazine, cocaine, crack, methamphetamine, and khat

What is their legal status in the United States?
Amphetamines are Schedule II stimulants, which means that they have a high potential for abuse and limited medical uses. Pharmaceutical products are available only through a prescription that cannot be refilled.

Cocaine

WHAT IS COCAINE?

Cocaine is an intense, euphoria-producing stimulant drug with strong addictive potential.

WHAT IS ITS ORIGIN?

Cocaine is derived from coca leaves grown in Bolivia, Peru, and Colombia. The cocaine manufacturing process takes place in remote jungle labs where the raw product undergoes a series of chemical transformations. Colombia produces about 90% of the cocaine powder reaching the United States. According to the 2005 Colombia Threat Assessment, 90% of the cocaine shipped to the United States comes from the Central America-Mexico corridor.

Cocaine powder

What are common street names?

Common street names include:

→ Coca, Coke, Crack, Flake, Snow, and Soda Cot

What does it look like?

Cocaine is usually distributed as a white, crystalline powder. Cocaine is often diluted ("cut") with a variety of substances, the most common of which are sugars and local anesthetics. It is "cut" to stretch the amount of the product and increase profits for dealers. In contrast, cocaine base (crack) looks like small, irregularly shaped chunks (or "rocks") of a whitish solid.

How is it abused?

Powdered cocaine can be snorted or injected into the veins after dissolving in water. Cocaine base (crack) is smoked, either alone or on marijuana or tobacco. Cocaine is also abused in combination with an opiate, like heroin, a practice known as "speedballing." Although injecting into veins or muscles, snorting, and smoking are the common ways of using cocaine, all mucous membranes readily absorb cocaine. Cocaine users typically binge on the drug until they are exhausted or run out of cocaine.

What is its effect on the mind?

The intensity of cocaine's euphoric effects depends on how quickly the drug reaches the brain, which depends on the dose and method of abuse. Following smoking or intravenous injection, cocaine reaches the brain in seconds, with a rapid buildup in levels. This results in a rapid-onset, intense euphoric effect known as a "rush."

By contrast, the euphoria caused by snorting cocaine is less intense and does not happen as quickly due to the slower build-up of the drug in the brain. Other effects include increased alertness and excitation, as well as restlessness, irritability, and anxiety.

Tolerance to cocaine's effects develops rapidly, causing users to take higher and higher doses. Taking high doses of cocaine or prolonged use, such as binging, usually causes paranoia. The crash that follows euphoria is characterized by mental and physical exhaustion, sleep, and depression lasting several days. Following the crash, users experience a craving to use cocaine again.

What is its effect on the body?

Physiological effects of cocaine include increased blood pressure and heart rate, dilated pupils, insomnia, and loss of appetite. The widespread abuse of highly pure street cocaine has led to many severe adverse health consequences such as:

→ Cardiac arrhythmias, ischemic heart conditions, sudden cardiac arrest, convulsions, strokes, and death

In some users, the long-term use of inhaled cocaine has led to a unique respiratory syndrome, and chronic snorting of cocaine has led to the erosion of the upper nasal cavity.

Which drugs cause similar effects?

Other stimulants, such as methamphetamine, cause effects similar to cocaine that vary mainly in degree.

What is its legal status in the United States?

Cocaine is a Schedule II drug under the Controlled Substances Act, meaning it has a high potential for abuse and limited medical usage. Cocaine hydrochloride solution (4% and 10%) is used primarily as a topical local anesthetic for the upper respiratory tract. It also is used to reduce bleeding of the mucous membranes in the mouth, throat, and nasal cavities. However, better products have been developed for these purposes, and cocaine is rarely used medically in the United States.

Cocaine bricks, seized by DEA

Khat

WHAT IS KHAT?

Khat is a flowering evergreen shrub that is abused for its stimulant-like effect. Khat has two active ingredients, cathine and cathinone.

WHAT IS ITS ORIGIN?

Khat is native to East Africa and the Arabian Peninsula, where the use of it is an established cultural tradition for many social situations

Khat plant

What are common street names?

Common street names for Khat include:

→ Abyssinian Tea, African Salad, Catha, Chat, Kat, and Oat

What does it look like?

Khat is a flowering evergreen shrub. Khat that is sold and abused is usually just the leaves, twigs, and shoots of the Khat shrub.

How is it abused?

Khat is typically chewed like tobacco, then retained in the cheek and chewed intermittently to release the active drug, which produces a stimulant-like effect. Dried Khat leaves can be made into tea or a chewable paste, and Khat can also be smoked and even sprinkled on food.

What is its effect on the mind?

Khat can induce manic behavior with:

→ Grandiose delusions, paranoia, nightmares, hallucinations, and hyperactivity

Chronic Khat abuse can result in violence and suicidal depression.

What is its effect on the body?

Khat causes an immediate increase in blood pressure and heart rate. Khat can also cause a brown staining of the teeth, insomnia, and gastric disorders. Chronic abuse of Khat can cause physical exhaustion.

What are its overdose effects?

The dose needed to constitute an overdose is not known, however it has historically been associated with those who have been long-term chewers of the leaves. Symptoms of toxicity include:

→ Delusions, loss of appetite, difficulty with breathing, and increases in both blood pressure and heart rate

Additionally, there are reports of liver damage (chemical hepatitis) and of cardiac complications, specifically myocardial infarctions. This mostly occurs among long-term chewers of khat or those who have chewed too large a dose.

Which drugs cause similar effects?

Khat's effects are similar to other stimulants, such as cocaine and methamphetamine.

What is its legal status in the United States?

The chemicals found in khat are controlled under the Controlled Substances Act. Cathine is a Schedule IV stimulant, and cathinone is a Schedule I stimulant under the Controlled Substances Act, meaning that it has a high potential for abuse, no currently accepted medical use in treatment in the United States, and a lack of accepted safety for use under medical supervision.

Methamphetamine

WHAT IS METHAMPHETAMINE?

Methamphetamine (meth) is a stimulant. The FDA-approved brand-name medication is Desoxyn®.

WHAT IS ITS ORIGIN?

Mexican drug trafficking organizations have become the primary manufacturers and distributors of methamphetamine to cities throughout the United States, including in Hawaii. Domestic clandestine laboratory operators also produce and distribute meth but usually on a smaller scale. The methods used depend on the availability of precursor chemicals.

Currently, meth is mainly made with diverted products that contain pseudoephedrine. The Combat Methamphetamine Epidemic Act of 2005 requires retailers of non-prescription products containing pseudoephedrine, ephedrine, or phenylpropanolamine to place these products behind the counter or in a locked cabinet. Consumers must show identification and sign a logbook for each purchase.

Methamphetamine in finished form.

What are common street names?

Common street names include:

→ Batu, Bikers Coffee, Black Beauties, Chalk, Chicken Feed, Crank, Crystal, Glass, Go-Fast, Hiropon, Ice, Meth, Methlies Quick, Poor Man's Cocaine, Shabu, Shards, Speed, Stove Top, Tina, Trash, Tweak, Uppers, Ventana, Vidrio, Yaba, and Yellow Bam

What does it look like?

Regular meth is a pill or powder. Crystal meth resembles glass fragments or shiny blue-white "rocks" of various sizes.

How is it abused?

Meth is swallowed, snorted, injected, or smoked. To intensify the effects, users may take higher doses of the drug, take it more frequently, or change their method of intake.

In some cases, meth abusers go without food and sleep while taking part in a form of binging known as a "run." Meth users on a "run" inject as much as a gram of the drug every two to three hours over several days until they run out of meth or become too disorganized to continue.

What is its effect on the mind?

Meth is a highly addictive drug with potent central nervous system (CNS) stimulant properties.

Those who smoke or inject it report a brief, intense sensation, or rush. Oral ingestion or snorting produces a long-lasting high instead of a rush, which reportedly can continue for as long as half a day. Both the rush and the high are believed to result from the release of very high levels of the neurotransmitter dopamine into areas of the brain that regulate feelings of pleasure.

Long-term meth use results in many damaging effects, including addiction.

Methamphetamine in finished form

Chronic meth abusers exhibit violent behavior, anxiety, confusion, insomnia, and psychotic features including paranoia, aggression, visual and auditory hallucinations, mood disturbances, and delusions — such as the sensation of insects creeping on or under the skin.

Such paranoia can result in homicidal or suicidal thoughts. Researchers have reported that as much as 50% of the dopamine-producing cells in the brain can be damaged after prolonged exposure to relatively low levels of meth. Researchers also have found that serotonin-containing nerve cells may be damaged even more extensively.

What is its effect on the body?

Taking even small amounts of meth can result in:

→ Increased wakefulness, increased physical activity, decreased appetite, rapid breathing and heart rate, irregular heartbeat, increased blood pressure, and hyperthermia (overheating)

High doses can elevate body temperature to dangerous, sometimes lethal, levels, and cause convulsions and even cardiovascular collapse and death. Meth abuse may also cause extreme anorexia, memory loss, and severe dental problems.

What are its overdose effects?

High doses may result in death from stroke, heart attack, or multiple organ problems caused by overheating.

Which drugs cause similar effects?

Cocaine and potent stimulant pharmaceuticals, such as amphetamines and methylphenidate, produce similar effects.

What is its legal status in the United States?

Methamphetamine is a Schedule II stimulant under the Controlled Substances Act, which means that it has a high potential for abuse and limited medical use. It is available only through a prescription that cannot be refilled. Today there is only one legal meth product, Desoxyn®. It is currently marketed in 5-milligram tablets and has very limited use in the treatment of obesity and attention deficit hyperactivity disorder (ADHD).

VII. Depressants

WHAT ARE DEPRESSANTS?

Depressants will put you to sleep, relieve anxiety and muscle spasms, and prevent seizures.

Barbiturates are older drugs and include butalbital (Fiorina®), phenobarbital, Pentothal®, Seconal® and Nembutal®. You can rapidly develop dependence on and tolerance to barbiturates, meaning you need more and more of them to feel and function normally. This makes them unsafe, increasing the likelihood of coma or death.

Benzodiazepines were developed to replace barbiturates, though they still share many of the undesirable side effects. Some examples are Valium®, Xanax®, Halcion®, Ativan®, Klonopin® and Restoril®. Rohypnol® is a benzodiazepine that is not manufactured or legally marketed in the United States, but it is used illegally.

Ambien® and Sonata® are sedative-hypnotic medications approved for the short-term treatment of insomnia that share many of the properties of benzodiazepines. Other CNS depressants include meprobamate, methaqualone (Quaalude®), and the illicit drug GHB.

WHAT IS THEIR ORIGIN?

Generally, legitimate pharmaceutical products are diverted to the illicit market. Teens can obtain depressants from the family medicine cabinet, friends, family members, the Internet, doctors, and hospitals.

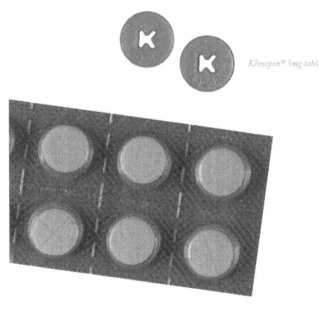

Klonopin® 5mg tablet

Blister pack of Rohypnol® tablets

What are common street names?
Common street names for depressants include:

→ Barbs, Benzos, Downers, Georgia Home Boy, GHB, Grievous Bodily Harm, Liquid X, Nerve Pills, Phennies, R2, Reds, Roofies, Rophies, Tranks, and Yellows

What do they look like?
Depressants come in the form of pills, syrups, and injectable liquids.

How are they abused?
Individuals abuse depressants to experience euphoria. Depressants are also used with other drugs to add to the other drugs' high or to deal with their side effects. Abusers take higher doses than people taking the drugs under a doctor's supervision for therapeutic purposes. Depressants like GHB and Rohypnol® are also misused to facilitate sexual assault.

What is their effect on the mind?

Depressants used therapeutically do what they are prescribed for:

→ to put you to sleep, relieve anxiety and muscle spasms, and prevent seizures

They also:

→ Cause amnesia, leaving no memory of events that occur while under the influence, reduce your reaction time, impair mental functioning and judgment, and cause confusion

Long-term use of depressants produces psychological dependence and tolerance.

What is their effect on the body?

Some depressants can relax the muscles. Unwanted physical effects include:

→ Slurred speech, loss of motor coordination, weakness, headache, lightheadedness, blurred vision, dizziness, nausea, vomiting, low blood pressure, and slowed breathing

Prolonged use of depressants can lead to physical dependence even at doses recommended for medical treatment. Unlike barbiturates, large doses of benzodiazepines are rarely fatal unless combined with other drugs or alcohol. But unlike the withdrawal syndrome seen with most other drugs of abuse, withdrawal from depressants can be life threatening.

What are their overdose effects?

High doses of depressants or use of them with alcohol or other drugs can slow heart rate and breathing enough to cause death.

Which drugs cause similar effects?

Some antipsychotics, antihistamines, and antidepressants produce sedative effects. Alcohol's effects are similar to those of depressants.

Vials containing GHB

What is their legal status in the United States?

Most depressants are controlled substances that range from Schedule I to Schedule IV under the Controlled Substances Act, depending on their risk for abuse and whether they currently have an accepted medical use. Many of the depressants have FDA-approved medical uses. Rohypnol® is not manufactured or legally marketed in the United States.

Barbiturates

WHAT ARE BARBITURATES?

Barbiturates are depressants that produce a wide spectrum of central nervous system depression from mild sedation to coma. They have also been used as sedatives, hypnotics, anesthetics, and anticonvulsants.

Barbiturates are classified as:
→ Ultrashort, Short, Intermediate, Long-acting

WHAT IS THEIR ORIGIN?

Barbiturates were first introduced for medical use in the 1900s, and today about 12 substances are in medical use.

What are common street names?
Common street names include:

→ Barbs, Block Busters, Christmas Trees, Goof Balls, Pinks, Red Devils, Reds & Blues, and Yellow Jackets

What do they look like?
Barbiturates come in a variety of multicolored pills and tablets. Abusers prefer the short-acting and intermediate barbiturates such as Amytal® and Seconal®.

How are they abused?
Barbiturates are abused by swallowing a pill or injecting a liquid form. Barbiturates are generally abused to reduce anxiety, decrease inhibitions, and treat unwanted effects of illicit drugs. Barbiturates can be extremely dangerous because overdoses can occur easily and lead to death.

What is their effect on the mind?
Barbiturates cause:

→ Mild euphoria, lack of inhibition, relief of anxiety, and sleepiness

Higher doses cause:

→ Impairment of memory, judgment, and coordination; irritability; and paranoid and suicidal ideation

Tolerance develops quickly and larger doses are then needed to produce the same effect, increasing the danger of an overdose.

What is their effect on the body?
Barbiturates slow down the central nervous system and cause sleepiness.

What are their overdose effects?
Effects of overdose include:

→ Shallow respiration, clammy skin, dilated pupils, weak and rapid pulse, coma, and possible death

Which drugs cause similar effects?
Drugs with similar effects include:

→ Alcohol, benzodiazepines like Valium® and Xanax®, tranquilizers, sleeping pills, Rohypnol®, and GHB

What is their legal status in the United States?
Barbiturates are Schedule II, III, and IV depressants under the Controlled Substances Act.

Benzodiazepines

WHAT ARE BENZODIAZEPINES?

Benzodiazepines are depressants that produce sedation, induce sleep, relieve anxiety and muscle spasms, and prevent seizures.

WHAT IS THEIR ORIGIN?

Benzodiazepines are only legally available through prescription. Many abusers maintain their drug supply by getting prescriptions from several doctors, forging prescriptions, or buying them illicitly. Alprazolam and diazepam are the two most frequently encountered benzodiazepines on the illicit market.

What are common street names?

Common street names include Benzos and Downers.

What do they look like?

The most common benzodiazepines are the prescription drugs Valium®, Xanax®, Halcion®, Ativan®, and Klonopin®. Tolerance can develop, although at variable rates and to different degrees. Shorter-acting benzodiazepines used to manage insomnia include estazolam (ProSom®), flurazepam (Dalmane®), temazepam (Restoril®), and triazolam (Halcion®). Midazolam (Versed®), a short-acting benzodiazepine, is utilized for sedation, anxiety, and amnesia in critical care settings and prior to anesthesia. It is available in the United States as an injectable preparation and as a syrup (primarily for pediatric patients).

Benzodiazepines with a longer duration of action are utilized to treat insomnia in patients with daytime anxiety. These benzodiazepines include alprazolam (Xanax®), chlordiazepoxide (Librium®), clorazepate (Tranxene®), diazepam (Valium®), halazepam (Paxipam®), lorzepam (Ativan®), oxazepam (Serax®), prazepam (Centrax®), and quazepam (Doral®). Clonazepam (Klonopin®), diazepam, and clorazepate are also used as anticonvulsants.

How are they abused?

Abuse is frequently associated with adolescents and young adults who take the drug orally or crush it up and snort it to get high. Abuse is particularly high among heroin and cocaine abusers.

What is their effect on the mind?

Benzodiazepines are associated with amnesia, hostility, irritability, and vivid or disturbing dreams.

What is their effect on the body?

Benzodiazepines slow down the central nervous system and may cause sleepiness.

What are their overdose effects?

Effects of overdose include:

→ Shallow respiration, clammy skin, dilated pupils, weak and rapid pulse, coma, and possible death

Which drugs cause similar effects?

Drugs that cause similar effects include:

→ Alcohol, barbiturates, sleeping pills, and GHB

What is their legal status in the United States?

Benzodiazepines are controlled in Schedule IV of the Controlled Substance Act.

GHB

WHAT IS GHB?

Gamma-Hydroxybutyric acid (GHB) is another name for the generic drug sodium oxybate. Xyrem® (which is sodium oxybate) is the trade name of the Food and Drug Administration (FDA)-approved prescription medication.

Analogues that are often substituted for GHB include GBL (gamma butyrolactone) and 1,4 BD (also called just "BD"), which is 1,4-butanediol. These analogues are available legally as industrial solvents used to produce polyurethane, pesticides, elastic fibers, pharmaceuticals, coatings on metal or plastic, and other products. They are also are sold illicitly as supplements for bodybuilding, fat loss, reversal of baldness, improved eyesight, and to combat aging, depression, drug addiction, and insomnia.

GBL and BD are sold as "fish tank cleaner," "ink stain re-mover," "ink cartridge cleaner" and "nail enamel remover" for approximately $100 per bottle — much more expensive than comparable products. Attempts to identify the abuse of GHB analogues are hampered by the fact that routine toxicological screens do not detect the presence of these analogues.

WHAT IS ITS ORIGIN?

GHB is produced illegally in both domestic and foreign clandestine laboratories. The major source of GHB on the street is through clandestine synthesis by local operators. At bars or "rave" parties, GHB is typically sold in liquid form by the capful or "swig" for $5 to $25 per cap. Xyrem® has the potential for diversion and abuse like any other pharmaceutical containing a controlled substance.

GHB has been encountered in nearly every region of the country.

What are common street names?

Common street names include:

→ Easy Lay, G, Georgia Home Boy, GHB, Goop, Grievous Bodily Harm, Liquid Ecstasy, Liquid X, and Scoop

What does it look like?

GHB is usually sold as a liquid or as a white powder that is dissolved in a liquid, such as water, juice, or alcohol. GHB dissolved in liquid has been packaged in small vials or small water bottles. In liquid form, GHB is clear and colorless and slightly salty in taste.

How is it abused?

GHB and its analogues are abused for their euphoric and calming effects and because some people believe they build muscles and cause weight loss.

GHB and its analogues are also misused for their ability to increase libido, suggestibility, passivity, and to cause amnesia (no memory of events while under the influence of the substance) — traits that make users vulnerable to sexual assault and other criminal acts.

GHB abuse became popular among teens and young adults at dance clubs and "raves" in the 1990s and gained notoriety as a date rape drug. GHB is taken alone or in combination with other drugs, such as alcohol (primarily), other depressants, stimulants, hallucinogens, and marijuana.

The average dose ranges from 1 to 5 grams (depending on the purity of the compound, this can be 1-2 teaspoons mixed in a beverage). However, the concentrations of these "home-brews" have varied so much that users are usually unaware of the actual dose they are drinking.

What is its effect on the mind?

GHB occurs naturally in the central nervous system in very small amounts. Use of GHB produces Central Nervous System (CNS) depressant effects including:

→ Euphoria, drowsiness, decreased anxiety, confusion, and memory impairment

GHB can also produce both visual hallucinations and — paradoxically — excited and aggressive behavior. GHB greatly increases the CNS depressant effects of alcohol and other depressants.

Vials containing GHB

What is its effect on the body?

GHB takes effect in 15 to 30 minutes, and the effects last 3 to 6 hours. Low doses of GHB produce nausea.

At high doses, GHB overdose can result in:

→ Unconsciousness, seizures, slowed heart rate, greatly slowed breathing, lower body temperature, vomiting, nausea, coma, and death

Regular use of GHB can lead to addiction and withdrawal that includes:

→ Insomnia, anxiety, tremors, increased heart rate and blood pressure, and occasional psychotic thoughts

Currently, there is no antidote available for GHB intoxication. GHB analogues are known to produce side effects such as:

→ Topical irritation to the skin and eyes, nausea, vomiting, incontinence, loss of consciousness, seizures, liver damage, kidney failure, respiratory depression, and death

What are its overdose effects?

GHB overdose can cause death.

Which drugs cause similar effects?

GHB analogues are often abused in place of GHB. Both GBL and BD metabolize to GHB when taken and produce effects similar to GHB.

CNS depressants such as barbiturates and methaqualone also produce effects similar to GHB.

What is its legal status in the United States?

GHB is a Schedule I controlled substance, meaning that it has a high potential for abuse, no currently accepted medical use in treatment in the United States, and a lack of accepted safety for use under medical supervision. GHB products are Schedule III substances under the Controlled Substances Act. In addition, GBL is a List I chemical.

It was placed on Schedule I of the Controlled Substances Act in March 2000. However, when sold as GHB products (such as Xyrem®), it is considered Schedule III, one of several drugs that are listed in multiple schedules.

Rohypnol®

WHAT IS ROHYPNOL®?

Rohypnol® is a trade name for flunitrazepam, a central nervous system (CNS) depressant that belongs to a class of drugs known as benzodiazepines. Flunitrazepam is also marketed as generic preparations and other trade name products outside of the United States.

Like other benzodiazepines, Rohypnol® produces sedative-hypnotic, anti-anxiety, and muscle relaxant effects. This drug has never been approved for medical use in the United States by the Food and Drug Administration. Outside the United States, Rohypnol® is commonly prescribed to treat insomnia. Rohypnol® is also referred to as a "date rape" drug.

WHAT IS ITS ORIGIN?

Rohypnol® is smuggled into the United States from other countries, such as Mexico.

What are common street names?

Common street names include:

→ Circles, Forget Pill, Forget-Me-Pill, La Rocha, Lunch Money Drug, Mexican Valium, Pingus, R2, Reynolds, Roach, Roach 2, Roaches, Roachies, Roapies, Robutal, Rochas Dos, Rohypnol, Roofies, Rophies, Ropies, Roples, Row-Shay, Ruffies, and Wolfies

What does it look like?

Prior to 1997, Rohypnol® was manufactured as a white tablet (0.5-2 milligrams per tablet), and when mixed in drinks, was colorless, tasteless, and odorless. In 1997, the manufacturer responded to concerns about the drug's role in sexual assaults by reformulating the drug.

Rohypnol® is now manufactured as an oblong olive green tablet with a speckled blue core that when dissolved in light-colored drinks will dye the liquid blue. However, generic versions of the drug may not contain the blue dye.

How is it abused?

The tablet can be swallowed whole, crushed and snorted, or dissolved in liquid. Adolescents may abuse Rohypnol® to produce a euphoric effect often described as a "high." While high, they experience reduced inhibitions and impaired judgment.

Rohypnol® is also abused in combination with alcohol to produce an exaggerated intoxication.

In addition, abuse of Rohypnol® may be associated with multiple-substance abuse. For example, cocaine addicts may use benzodiazepines such as Rohypnol® to relieve the side effects (e.g., irritability and agitation) associated with cocaine binges.

Rohypnol® is also misused to physically and psychologically incapacitate women targeted for sexual assault. The drug is usually placed in the alcoholic drink of an unsuspecting victim to incapacitate them and prevent resistance to sexual assault. The drug leaves the victim unaware of what has happened to them.

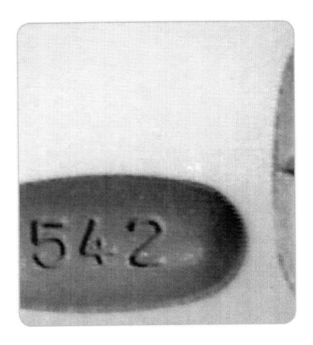

Rohypnol® tablets

What is its effect on the mind?

Like other benzodiazepines, Rohypnol® slows down the functioning of the CNS producing:

→ Drowsiness (sedation), sleep (pharmacological hypnosis), decreased anxiety, and amnesia (no memory of events while under the influence of the substance)

Rohypnol® can also cause:

→ Increased or decreased reaction time, impaired mental functioning and judgment, confusion, aggression, and excitability

What is its effect on the body?

Rohypnol® causes muscle relaxation. Adverse physical effects include:

→ Slurred speech, loss of motor coordination, weakness, headache, and respiratory depression

Rohypnol also can produce physical dependence when taken regularly over a period of time.

What are its overdose effects?

High doses of Rohypnol®, particularly when combined with CNS depressant drugs such as alcohol and heroin, can cause severe sedation, unconsciousness, slow heart rate, and suppression of respiration that may be sufficient to result in death.

Which drugs cause similar effects?

Drugs that cause similar effects include GHB (gamma hydroxybutyrate) and other benzodiazepines such as alprazolam (e.g., Xanax®), clonazepam (e.g., Klonopin®), and diazepam (e.g., Valium®).

What is its legal status in the United States?

Rohypnol® is a Schedule IV substance under the Controlled Substance Act. Rohypnol® is not approved for manufacture, sale, use or importation to the United States. It is legally manufactured and marketed in many countries. Penalties for possession, trafficking, and distribution involving one gram or more are the same as those of a Schedule I drug.

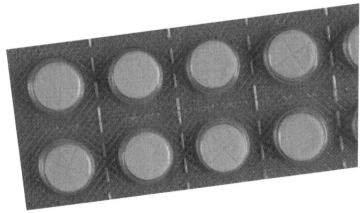

Blister pack of Rohypnol® tablets

VIII. Hallucinogens

WHAT ARE HALLUCINOGENS?

Hallucinogens are found in plants and fungi or are synthetically produced and are among the oldest known group of drugs used for their ability to alter human perception and mood.

WHAT IS THEIR ORIGIN?

Hallucinogens can be synthetically produced in illicit laboratories or are found in plants.

MDMA/Ecstasy pills

LSD Blotter Sheet

What are common street names?

Common street names include:

→ Acid, Blotter, Blotter Acid, Cubes, Doses, Fry, Mind Candy, Mushrooms, Shrooms, Special K, STP, X, and XTC

What do they look like?

Hallucinogens come in a variety of forms. MDMA or ecstasy tablets are sold in many colors with a variety of logos to attract young abusers. LSD is sold in the form of impregnated paper (blotter acid), typically imprinted with colorful graphic designs.

How are they abused?

The most commonly abused halluncinogens among junior and senior high school students are hallucinogenic mushrooms, LSD, and MDMA or ecstasy. Hallucinogens are typically taken orally or can be smoked.

What is their effect on the mind?

Sensory effects include perceptual distortions that vary with dose, setting, and mood. Psychic effects include distortions of thought associated with time and space. Time may appear to stand still, and forms and

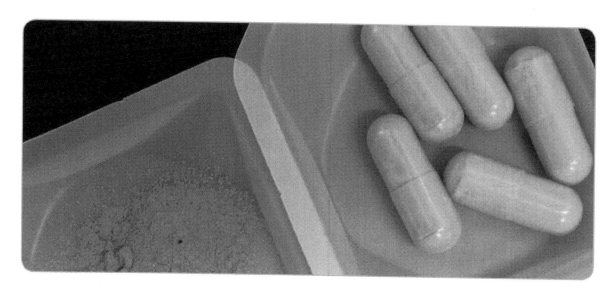

LSD powder and capsules

colors seem to change and take on new significance. Weeks or even months after some hallucinogens have been taken, the user may experience flashbacks — fragmentary recurrences of certain aspects of the drug experience in the absence of actually taking the drug. The occurrence of a flashback is unpredictable, but is more likely to occur during times of stress and seems to occur more frequently in younger individuals. With time, these episodes diminish and become less intense.

What is their effect on the body?

Physiological effects include elevated heart rate, increased blood pressure, and dilated pupils.

What are their overdose effects?

Deaths exclusively from acute overdose of LSD, magic mushrooms, and mescaline are extremely rare. Deaths generally occur due to suicide, accidents, and dangerous behavior, or due to the person inadvertently eating poisonous plant material.

A severe overdose of PCP and ketamine can result in:

→ Respiratory depression, coma, convulsions, seizures, and death due to respiratory arrest

What is their legal status in the United States?

Many hallucinogens are Schedule I under the Controlled Substances Act, meaning that they have a high potential for abuse, no currently accepted medical use in treatment in the United States, and a lack of accepted safety for use under medical supervision.

Ecstasy/MDMA

WHAT IS ECSTASY/MDMA?

MDMA acts as both a stimulant and psychedelic, producing an energizing effect, distortions in time and perception, and enhanced enjoyment of tactile experiences.

Adolescents and young adults use it to reduce inhibitions and to promote:

→ Euphoria, feelings of closeness, empathy, and sexuality

Although MDMA is known among users as Ecstasy, researchers have determined that many Ecstasy tablets contain not only MDMA but also a number of other drugs or drug combinations that can be harmful, such as:

→ Methamphetamine, ketamine, cocaine, the over-the-counter cough suppressant dextromethorphan (DXM), the diet drug ephedrine, and caffeine

In addition, other drugs similar to MDMA, such as MDA or PMA, are often sold as Ecstasy, which can lead to overdose and death when the user takes additional doses to obtain the desired effect.

WHAT IS ITS ORIGIN?

MDMA is a synthetic chemical made in labs. Seized MDMA in the U.S. is primarily manufactured in, and smuggled across our borders from, clandestine laboratories in Canada and, to a lesser extent, the Netherlands. A small number of MDMA clandestine laboratories have also been identified operating in the U.S.

What are common street names?

Common street names include:

→ Adam, Beans, Clarity, Disco Biscuit, E, Ecstasy, Eve, Go, Hug Drug, Lover's Speed, MDMA, Peace, STP, X, and XTC

What does it look like?

MDMA is mainly distributed in tablet form. MDMA tablets are sold with logos, creating brand names for users to seek out. The colorful pills are often hidden among colorful candies. MDMA is also distributed in capsules, powder, and liquid forms.

How is it abused?

MDMA use mainly involves swallowing tablets (50-150 mg), which are sometimes crushed and snorted, occasionally smoked but rarely injected. MDMA is also available as a powder.

MDMA abusers usually take MDMA by "stacking" (taking three or more tablets at once) or by "piggy-backing" (taking a series of tablets over a short period of time). One trend among young adults is "candy flipping," which is the co-abuse of MDMA and LSD.

MDMA is considered a "party drug." As with many other drugs of abuse, MDMA is rarely used alone. It is common for users to mix MDMA with other substances, such as alcohol and marijuana.

What is its effect on the mind?

MDMA mainly affects brain cells that use the chemical serotonin to communicate with each other. Serotonin helps to regulate mood, aggression, sexual activity, sleep, and sensitivity to pain. Clinical studies suggest that MDMA may increase the risk of long-term, perhaps permanent, problems with memory and learning.

MDMA causes changes in perception, including euphoria and increased sensitivity to touch, energy, sensual and sexual arousal, need to be touched, and need for stimulation.

Some unwanted psychological effects include:

→ Confusion, anxiety, depression, paranoia, sleep problems, and drug craving

All these effects usually occur within 30 to 45 minutes of swallowing the drug and usually last 4 to 6 hours, but they may occur or last weeks after ingestion.

What is its effect on the body?

Users of MDMA experience many of the same effects and face many of the same risks as users of other stimulants such as cocaine and amphetamines. These include increased motor activity, alertness, heart rate, and blood pressure.

MDMA/Ecstasy pills

Some unwanted physical effects include:

→ Muscle tension, tremors, involuntary teeth clenching, muscle cramps, nausea, faintness, chills, sweating, and blurred vision

High doses of MDMA can interfere with the ability to regulate body temperature, resulting in a sharp increase in body temperature (hyperthermia), leading to liver, kidney and cardiovascular failure.

Severe dehydration can result from the combination of the drug's effects and the crowded and hot conditions in which the drug is often taken.

Studies suggest chronic use of MDMA can produce damage to the serotonin system. It is ironic that a drug that is taken to increase pleasure may cause damage that reduces a person's ability to feel pleasure.

What are its overdose effects?

In high doses, MDMA can interfere with the body's ability to regulate temperature. On occasions, this can lead to a sharp increase in body temperature (hyperthermia), resulting in liver, kidney, and cardiovascular system failure, and death. Because MDMA can interfere with its own metabolism (that is, its break down within the body), potentially harmful levels can be reached by repeated drug use within short intervals.

Which drugs cause similar effects?

No one other drug is quite like MDMA, but MDMA produces both amphetamine-like stimulation and m ld mescaline-like hallucinations.

What is its legal status in the United States?

MDMA is a Schedule I drug under the Controlled Substances Act, meaning it has a high potential for abuse, no currently accepted medical use in treatment in the United States, and a lack of accepted safety for use under medical supervision.

K2/Spice

WHAT IS K2?

K2 or "Spice" is a mixture of herbs and spices that is typically sprayed with a synthetic compound chemically similar to THC, the psychoactive ingredients in marijuana. The chemical compounds typically include HU-210, HU-211, JWH-018, and JWH-073. K2 is commonly purchased in head shops, tobacco shops, various retail outlets, and over the Internet. It is often marketed as incense or "fake weed." Purchasing over the Internet can be dangerous because it is not usually known where the products come from or what amount of chemical is on the organic material.

WHAT IS ITS ORIGIN?

Manufacturers of this product are not regulated and are often unknown since these products are purchased via the Internet whether wholesale or retail. Several websites that sell the product are based in China. Some products may contain an herb called damiana, which is native to Central America, Mexico, and the Caribbean.

What are common street names?

→ Bilss, Black Mamba, Bombay Blue, Fake Weed, Genie, Spice, Zohai

What does it look like?

K2 is typically sold in small, silvery plastic bags of dried leaves and marketed as incense that can be smoked. It is said to resemble potpourri.

How is it abused?

K2 products are usually smoked in joints or pipes, but some users make it into a tea.

What is its effect on the mind?

Psychological effects are similar to those of marijuana and include paranoia, panic attacks, and giddiness.

What is its effect on the body?

Physiological effects of K2 include increased heart rate and increase of blood pressure. It appears to be stored in the body for long periods of time, and therefore the long-term effects on humans are not fully known.

What are its overdose effects?

There have been no reported deaths by overdose.

Which drugs cause similar effects?

Marijuana

What is its legal status in the United States?

On Tuesday, March 1, 2011, DEA published a final order in the Federal Register temporarily placing five synthetic cannabinoids into Schedule I of the CSA. The order became effective on March 1, 2011.

The substances placed into Schedule I are 1-pentyl-3-(1-naphthoyl) indole (JWH-018), 1-butyl-3-(1-naphthoyl) indole (JWH-073), 1-[2-(4-morpholinyl)ethyl]-3-(1-naphthoyl)indole (JWH-200), 5-(1,1-dimethylheptyl)-2-[(1R,3S)-3-hydroxycyclohexyl]-phenol (CP-47,497), and 5-(1,1-dimethyloctyl)-2-[(1R,3S)-3-hydroxycyclohexyl]-phenol (cannabicyclohexanol; CP-47,497 C8 homologue).

This action is based on a finding by the Administrator that the placement of these synthetic cannabinoids into Schedule I of the CSA is necessary to avoid an imminent hazard to the public safety. As a result of this order, the full effect of the CSA and its implementing regulations including criminal, civil and administrative penalties, sanctions, and regulatory controls of Schedule I substances will be imposed on the manufacture, distribution, possession, importation, and exportation of these synthetic cannabinoids.

Ketamine

WHAT IS KETAMINE?

Ketamine is a dissociative anesthetic that has some hallucinogenic effects. It distorts perceptions of sight and sound and makes the user feel disconnected and not in control. It is an injectable, short-acting anesthetic for use in humans and animals. It is referred to as a "dissociative anesthetic" because it makes patients feel detached from their pain and environment.

Ketamine can induce a state of sedation (feeling calm and relaxed), immobility, relief from pain, and amnesia (no memory of events while under the influence of the drug). It is abused for its ability to produce dissociative sensations and hallucinations. Ketamine has also been used to facilitate sexual assault.

WHAT IS ITS ORIGIN?

Ketamine is produced commercially in a number of countries, including the United States. Most of the ketamine illegally distributed in the United States is diverted or stolen from legitimate sources, particularly veterinary clinics, or smuggled into the United States from Mexico.

Distribution of ketamine typically occurs among friends and acquaintances, most often at raves, nightclubs, and at private parties; street sales of ketamine are rare.

What are common street names?

Common street names include:

→ Cat Tranquilizer, Cat Valium, Jet K, Kit Kat, Purple, Special K, Special La Coke, Super Acid, Super K, and Vitamin K

What does it look like?

Ketamine comes in a clear liquid and a white or off-white powder. Powdered ketamine (100 milligrams to 200 milligrams) typically is packaged in small glass vials, small plastic bags, and capsules as well as paper, glassine, or aluminum foil folds.

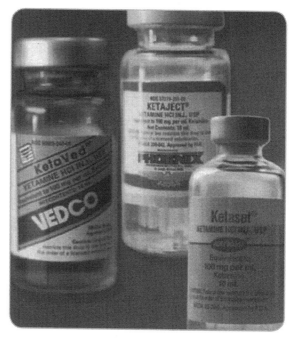

Vials containing liquid ketamine

How is it abused?

Ketamine, along with the other "club drugs," has become popular among teens and young adults at dance clubs and "raves." Ketamine is manufactured commercially as a powder or liquid. Powdered ketamine is also formed from pharmaceutical ketamine by evaporating the liquid using hot plates, warming trays, or microwave ovens, a process that results in the formation of crystals, which are then ground into powder.

Powdered ketamine is cut into lines known as bumps and snorted, or it is smoked, typically in marijuana or tobacco cigarettes. Liquid ketamine is injected or mixed into drinks. Ketamine is found by itself or often in combination with MDMA, amphetamine, methamphetamine, or cocaine.

What is its effect on the mind?

Ketamine produces hallucinations. It distorts perceptions of sight and sound and makes the user feel disconnected and not in control. A "Special K" trip is touted as better than that of LSD or PCP because its hallucinatory effects are relatively short in duration, lasting approximately 30 to 60 minutes as opposed to several hours.

Slang for experiences related to Ketamine or effects of Ketamine include:

→ "K-land" (refers to a mellow & colorful experience)

→ "K-hole" (refers to the out-of-body, near death experience)

→ "Baby food" (users sink in to blissful, infantile inertia)

→ "God" (users are convinced that they have met their maker)

The onset of effects is rapid and often occurs within a few minutes of taking the drug, though taking it orally results in a slightly slower onset of effects. Flashbacks have been reported several weeks after ketamine is used. Ketamine may also cause agitation, depression, cognitive difficulties, unconsciousness, and amnesia.

What is its effect on the body?
A couple of minutes after taking the drug, the user may experience an increase in heart rate and blood pressure that gradually decreases over the next 10 to 20 minutes. Ketamine can make users unresponsive to stimuli. When in this state, users experience:

→ Involuntarily rapid eye movement, dilated pupils, salivation, tear secretions, and stiffening of the muscles

This drug can also cause nausea.

What are its overdose effects?
An overdose can cause unconsciousness and dangerously slowed breathing.

Which drugs cause similar effects?
Other hallucinogenic drugs such as LSD, PCP, and mescaline can cause hallucinations. There are also several drugs such as GHB, Rohypnol and other depressants that are misused for their amnesiac or sedative properties to facilitate sexual assault.

Ketamine in various forms

What is its legal status in the United States?
Since the 1970s, ketamine has been marketed in the United States as an injectable, short-acting anesthetic for use in humans and animals. In 1999, ketamine including its salts, isomers, and salts of isomers, became a Schedule III non-narcotic substance under the Federal Controlled Substances Act. It has a currently acceptable medical use but some potential for abuse, which may lead to moderate or low physical dependence or high psychological dependence.

LSD

WHAT IS LSD?

LSD is a potent hallucinogen that has a high potential for abuse, but currently has an accepted medical use in treatment in the United States.

WHAT IS ITS ORIGIN?

LSD is produced in clandestine laboratories in the United States.

What are common street names?

Common names for LSD include:

→ Acid, Blotter Acid, Dots, Mellow Yellow, and Window Pane

What does it look like?

LSD is sold on the street in tablets, capsules, and occasionally in liquid form. It is an odorless and colorless substance with a slightly bitter taste. LSD is often added to absorbent paper, such as blotter paper, and divided into small decorated squares, with each square representing one dose.

How is it abused?

LSD is abused orally.

What is its effect on the mind?

During the first hour after ingestion, users may experience visual changes with extreme changes in mood. While hallucinating, the user may suffer impaired depth and time perception accompanied by distorted perception of the shape and size of objects, movements, colors, sound, touch and the user's own body image.

The ability to make sound judgments and see common dangers is impaired, making the user susceptible to personal injury. It is possible for users to suffer acute anxiety and depression after an LSD "trip" and flashbacks have been reported days, and even months, after taking the last dose.

LSD powder

What is its effect on the body?

The physical effects include:

→ Dilated pupils, higher body temperature, increased heart rate and blood pressure, sweating, loss of appetite, sleeplessness, dry mouth, and tremors

What are its overdose effects?

Longer, more intense "trip" episodes, psychosis, and possible death

Which drugs cause similar effects?

LSD's effects are similar to other hallucinogens, such as PCP, mescaline, and peyote.

What is its legal status in the United States?

LSD is a Schedule I substance under the Controlled Substances Act, meaning that it has a high potential for abuse, no currently accepted medical use in treatment in the United States, and a lack of accepted safety for use under medical supervision.

Peyote & Mescaline

WHAT ARE PEYOTE AND MESCALINE?

Peyote is a small, spineless cactus. The active ingredient in peyote is the hallucinogen mescaline.

WHAT IS ITS ORIGIN?

From earliest recorded time, peyote has been used by natives in northern Mexico and the southwestern United States as a part of their religious rites. Mescaline can be extracted from peyote or produced synthetically.

What are common street names?

Common street names include:

→ Buttons, Cactus, Mesc, and Peyoto

What does it look like?

The top of the peyote cactus is referred to as the "crown" and consists of disc-shaped buttons that are cut off.

How is it abused?

The fresh or dried buttons are chewed or soaked in water to produce an intoxicating liquid. Peyote buttons may also be ground into a powder that can be placed inside gelatin capsules to be swallowed, or smoked with a leaf material such as cannabis or tobacco.

What is its effect on the mind?

Abuse of peyote and mescaline will cause varying degrees of:

→ Illusions, hallucinations, altered perception of space and time, and altered body image

Users may also experience euphoria, which is sometimes followed by feelings of anxiety.

What is its effect on the body?

Following the consumption of peyote and mescaline, users may experience:

→ Intense nausea, vomiting, dilation of the pupils, increased heart rate, increased blood pressure, a rise in body temperature that causes heavy perspiration, headaches, muscle weakness, and impaired motor coordination

Which drugs cause similar effects?

Other hallucinogens like LSD, psilocybin (mushrooms), and PCP

What is its legal status in the United States?

Peyote and Mescaline are Schedule I substances under the Controlled Substances Act, meaning that they have a high potential for abuse, no currently accepted medical use in treatment in the United States, and a lack of accepted safety for use under medical supervision.

Peyote cactus

Psilocybin

WHAT IS PSILOCYBIN?

Psilocybin is a chemical obtained from certain types of fresh or dried mushrooms.

WHAT IS ITS ORIGIN?

Psilocybin mushrooms are found in Mexico, Central America, and the United States.

What are common street names?

Common street names include:

→ Magic Mushrooms, Mushrooms, and Shrooms

What does it look like?

Mushrooms containing psilocybin are available fresh or dried and have long, slender stems topped by caps with dark gills on the underside. Fresh mushrooms have white or whitish-gray stems; the caps are dark brown around the edges and light brown or white in the center. Dried mushrooms are usually rusty brown with isolated areas of off-white.

How is it abused?

Psilocybin mushrooms are ingested orally. They may also be brewed as a tea or added to other foods to mask their bitter flavor.

What is its effect on the mind?

The psychological consequences of psilocybin use include hallucinations and an inability to discern fantasy from reality. Panic reactions and psychosis also may occur, particularly if a user ingests a large dose.

What is its effect on the body?

The physical effects include:

→ Nausea, vomiting, muscle weakness, and lack of coordination

Psilocybin mushrooms

What are its overdose effects?

Effects of overdose include:

→ Longer, more intense "trip" episodes, psychosis, and possible death

Abuse of psilocybin mushrooms could also lead to poisoning if one of the many varieties of poisonous mushrooms is incorrectly identified as a psilocybin mushroom.

Which drugs cause similar effects?

Psilocybin effects are similar to other hallucinogens, such as mescaline and peyote.

What is its legal status in the United States?

Psilocybin is a Schedule I substance under the Controlled Substances Act, meaning that it has a high potential for abuse, no currently accepted medical use in treatment in the United States, and a lack of accepted safety for use under medical supervision.

IX. Marijuana/Cannabis

WHAT IS MARIJUANA?

Marijuana is a mind-altering (psychoactive) drug, produced by the Cannabis sativa plant. Marijuana contains over 480 constituents. THC (delta-9-tetrahydrocannabinol) is believed to be the main ingredient that produces the psychoactive effect.

WHAT IS ITS ORIGIN?

Marijuana is grown in the United States, Canada, Mexico, South America, and Asia. It can be cultivated in both outdoor and in indoor settings.

What are common street names?

Common street names include:

→ Aunt Mary, BC Bud, Blunts, Boom, Chronic, Dope, Gangster, Ganja, Grass, Hash, Herb, Hydro, Indo, Joint, Kif, Mary Jane, Mota, Pot, Reefer, Sinsemilla, Skunk, Smoke, Weed, and Yerba

What does it look like?

Marijuana is a dry, shredded green/brown mix of flowers, stems, seeds, and leaves from the Cannabis sativa plant. The mixture typically is green, brown, or gray in color and may resemble tobacco.

How is it abused?

Marijuana is usually smoked as a cigarette (called a joint) or in a pipe or bong. It is also smoked in blunts, which are cigars that have been emptied of tobacco and refilled with marijuana, sometimes in combination with another drug. Marijuana is also mixed with foods or brewed as a tea.

What is its effect on the mind?

When marijuana is smoked, the THC passes from the lungs and into the bloodstream, which carries the chemical to the organs throughout the body, including the brain. In the brain, the THC connects to specific sites called cannabinoid receptors on nerve cells and influences the activity of those cells.

Many of these receptors are found in the parts of the brain that influence:

→ Pleasure, memory, thought, concentration, sensory and time perception, and coordinated movement

The short-term effects of marijuana include:

→ Problems with memory and learning, distorted perception, difficulty in thinking and problem-solving, and loss of coordination

The effect of marijuana on perception and coordination are responsible for serious impairments in learning, associative processes, and psychomotor behavior (driving abilities). Long term, regular use can lead to physical dependence and withdrawal following discontinuation, as well as psychic addiction or dependence.

Clinical studies show that the physiological, psychological, and behavioral effects of marijuana vary among individuals and present a list of common responses to cannabinoids, as described in the scientific literature:

→ Dizziness, nausea, tachycardia, facial flushing, dry mouth and tremor initially

→ Merriment, happiness, and even exhilaration at high doses

→ Disinhibition, relaxation, increased sociability, and talkativeness

→ Enhanced sensory perception, giving rise to increased appreciation of music, art, and touch

→ Heightened imagination leading to a subjective sense of increased creativity

→ Time distortions

→ Illusions, delusions, and hallucinations are rare except at high doses

→ Impaired judgment, reduced coordination, and ataxia, which can impede driving ability or lead to an increase in risk-taking behavior

→ Emotional lability, incongruity of affect, dysphoria, disorganized thinking, inability to converse logically, agitation, paranoia, confusion, restlessness, anxiety, drowsiness, and panic attacks may occur, especially in inexperienced users or in those who have taken a large dose

→ Increased appetite and short-term memory impairment are common

Researchers have also found an association between marijuana use and an increased risk of depression, an increased risk and earlier onset of schizophrenia, and other psychotic disorders, especially for teens that have a genetic predisposition.

What is its effect on the body?

Short-term physical effects from marijuana use may include:

→ Sedation, blood shot eyes, increased heart rate, coughing from lung irritation, increased appetite, and decreased blood pressure

Like tobacco smokers, marijuana smokers experience serious health problems such as bronchitis, emphysema, and bronchial asthma. Extended use may cause suppression of the immune system. Because marijuana contains toxins and carcinogens, marijuana smokers increase their risk of cancer of the head, neck, lungs, and respiratory tract.

Withdrawal from chronic use of high doses of marijuana causes physical signs including headache, shakiness, sweating, and stomach pains and nausea.

Withdrawal symptoms also include behavioral signs such as:

→ Restlessness, irritability, sleep difficulties, and decreased appetite

Leaf of marijuana plant

What are its overdose effects?

No death from overdose of marijuana has been reported.

Which drugs cause similar effects?

Hashish and hashish oil are drugs made from the cannabis plant that are like marijuana, only stronger.

Hashish (hash) consists of the THC-rich resinous material of the cannabis plant, which is collected, dried, and then compressed into a variety of forms, such as balls, cakes, or cookie like sheets. Pieces are then broken off, placed in pipes or mixed with tobacco and placed in pipes or cigarettes, or smoked.

The main sources of hashish are the Middle East, North Africa, Pakistan, and Afghanistan.

Hashish Oil (hash oil, liquid hash, cannabis oil) is produced by extracting the cannabinoids from the plant material with a solvent. The color and odor of the extract will vary, depending on the solvent used. A drop or two of this liquid on a cigarette is equal to a single marijuana joint. Like marijuana, hashish and hashish oil are both Schedule I drugs.

What is its legal status in the United States?

Marijuana is a Schedule I substance under the Controlled Substances Act, meaning that it has a high potential for abuse, no currently accepted medical use in treatment in the United States, and a lack of accepted safety for use under medical supervision.

Marinol, a synthetic version of THC, the active ingredient found in the marijuana plant, can be prescribed for the control of nausea and vomiting caused by chemotherapeutic agents used in the treatment of cancer and to stimulate appetite in AIDS patients. Marinol is a Schedule III substance under the Controlled Substances Act.

X. Steroids

WHAT ARE STEROIDS?

Anabolic steroids are synthetically produced variants of the naturally occurring male hormone testosterone that are abused in an attempt to promote muscle growth, enhance athletic or other physical performance, and improve physical appearance.

Testosterone, nandrolone, stanozolol,methandienone, and boldenone are some of the most frequently abused anabolic steroids.

WHAT IS THEIR ORIGIN?

Most illicit steroids are smuggled into the U.S. from abroad. Steroids are also illegally diverted from legitimate sources (theft or inappropriate prescribing). The Internet is the most widely used means of buying and selling anabolic steroids. Steroids are also bought and sold at gyms, bodybuilding competitions, and schools from teammates, coaches, and trainers.

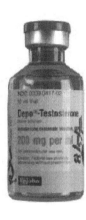

Depo-Testosterone

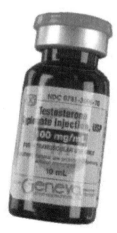

Testosterone Cypionate Injection, USB

What are common street names?

Common street names include:

→ Arnolds, Juice, Pumpers, Roids, Stackers, and Weight Gainers

What do they look like?

Steroids are available in:

→ Tablets and capsules, sublingual-tablets, liquid drops, gels, creams, transdermal patches, subdermal implant pellets, and water-based and oil-based injectable solutions

The appearance of these products varies depending on the type and manufacturer.

How are they abused?

Steroids are ingested orally, injected intramuscularly, or applied to the skin. The doses abused are often 10 to 100 times higher than the approved therapeutic and medical treatment dosages. Users typically take two or more anabolic steroids at the same time in a cyclic manner, believing that this will improve their effectiveness and minimize the adverse effects.

What is their effect on the mind?

Case studies and scientific research indicate that high doses of anabolic steroids may cause mood and behavioral effects.

In some individuals, steroid use can cause dramatic mood swings, increased feelings of hostility, impaired judgment, and increased levels of aggression (often referred to as "roid rage")

When users stop taking steroids, they may experience depression that may be severe enough to lead one to commit suicide. Anabolic steroid use may also cause psychological dependence and addiction.

What is their effect on the body?

A wide range of adverse effects is associated with the use or abuse of anabolic steroids. These effects depend on several factors including:

→ Age, sex, the anabolic steroid used, amount used, and duration of use

In adolescents, anabolic steroid use can stunt the ultimate height that an individual achieves.

In boys, steroid use can cause early sexual development, acne, and stunted growth.

In adolescent girls and women, anabolic steroid use can induce permanent physical changes, such as deepening of the voice, increased facial and body hair growth, menstrual irregularities, male pattern baldness, and lengthening of the clitoris.

In men, anabolic steroid use can cause shrinkage of the testicles, reduced sperm count, enlargement of the male breast tissue, sterility, and an increased risk of prostate cancer.

In both men and women, anabolic steroid use can cause high cholesterol levels, which may increase the risk of coronary artery disease, strokes, and heart attacks. Anabolic steroid use can also cause acne and fluid retention. Oral preparations of anabolic steroids, in particular, can damage the liver.

Abusers who inject steroids run the risk of contracting various infections due to non-sterile injection techniques, sharing of contaminated needles, and the use of steroid preparations manufactured in non-sterile environments. All these factors put users at risk for contracting viral infections such as HIV/AIDS or hepatitis B or C, and bacterial infections at the sight of injection.

Abusers may also develop endocarditis, a bacterial infection that causes a potentially fatal inflammation of the heart lining.

What are their overdose effects?

Anabolic steroids are not associated with overdoses. The adverse effects a user would experience develop from the use of steroids over time.

Which drugs cause similar effects?

There are several substances that produce effects similar to those of anabolic steroids. These include human growth hormone (hHG), clenbuterol, gonadotropins, and erythropoietin.

What is their legal status in the United States?

Anabolic steroids are Schedule III substances under the Controlled Substances Act. Only a small number of anabolic steroids are approved for either human or veterinary use. Steroids may be prescribed by a licensed physician for the treatment of testosterone deficiency, delayed puberty, low red blood cell count, breast cancer, and tissue wasting resulting from AIDS.

XI. Inhalants

WHAT ARE INHALANTS?

Inhalants are invisible, volatile substances found in common household products that produce chemical vapors that are inhaled to induce psychoactive or mind altering effects.

WHAT IS THEIR ORIGIN?

There are more than 1,000 products that are very dangerous when inhaled — things like typewriter correction fluid, air conditioning refrigerant, felt tip markers, spray paint, air freshener, butane, and even cooking spray. See products abused as inhalants at **www.inhalants.org/product.htm** (National Inhalant Prevention Coalition).

Highlighter markers

Paint thinner

What are common street names?
Common street names include:

→ Gluey, Huff, Rush, and Whippets

What do they look like?
Common household products such as glue, lighter fluid, cleaning fluids, and paint all produce chemical vapors that can be inhaled.

How are they abused?
Although other abused substances can be inhaled, the term "inhalants" is used to describe a variety of substances whose main common characteristic is that they are rarely, if ever, taken by any route other than inhalation.

Inhalants are breathed in through the nose or the mouth in a variety of ways, such as:

→ "Sniffing" or "snorting"

→ "Bagging" — sniffing or inhaling fumes from substances sprayed or deposited inside a plastic or paper bag

→ "Huffing" from an inhalant-soaked rag stuffed in the mouth, or inhaling from balloons filled with nitrous oxide

Inhalants are often among the first drugs that young children use. About 1 in 5 kids report having used inhalants by the eighth grade. Inhalants are also one of the few substances abused more by younger children than by older ones.

What is their effect on the mind?

Inhalant abuse can cause damage to the parts of the brain that control thinking, moving, seeing, and hearing. Cognitive abnormalities can range from mild impairment to severe dementia.

What is their effect on the body?

Inhaled chemicals are rapidly absorbed through the lungs into the bloodstream and quickly distributed to the brain and other organs. Nearly all inhalants produce effects similar to anesthetics, which slow down the body's function. Depending on the degree of abuse, the user can experience slight stimulation, feeling of less inhibition or loss of consciousness.

Within minutes of inhalation, the user experiences intoxication along with other effects similar to those produced by alcohol. These effects may include slurred speech, an inability to coordinate movements, euphoria, and dizziness. After heavy use of inhalants, abusers may feel drowsy for several hours and experience a lingering headache.

Additional symptoms exhibited by long-term inhalant abusers include:

→ Weight loss, muscle weakness, disorientation, inattentiveness, lack of coordination, irritability, depression, and damage to the nervous system and other organs

Some of the damaging effects to the body may be at least partially reversible when inhalant abuse is stopped; however, many of the effects from prolonged abuse are irreversible.

Prolonged sniffing of the highly concentrated chemicals in solvents or aerosol sprays can induce irregular and rapid heart rhythms and lead to heart failure and death within minutes. There is a common link between inhalant use and problems in school — failing grades, chronic absences, and general apathy.

Other signs include:

→ Paint or stains on body or clothing; spots or sores around the mouth; red or runny eyes or nose; chemical breath odor; drunk, dazed, or dizzy appearance; nausea; loss of appetite; anxiety; excitability; and irritability

What are their overdose effects?

Because intoxication lasts only a few minutes, abusers try to prolong the high by continuing to inhale repeatedly over the course of several hours, which is a very dangerous practice. With successive inhalations, abusers may suffer loss of consciousness and/or death.

"Sudden sniffing death" can result from a single session of inhalant use by an otherwise healthy young person. Sudden sniffing death is particularly associated with the abuse of butane, propane, and chemicals in aerosols.

Inhalant abuse can also cause death by asphyxiation from repeated inhalations, which lead to high concentrations of inhaled fumes displacing the available oxygen in the lungs, suffocation by blocking air from entering the lungs when inhaling fumes from a plastic bag placed over the head, and choking from swallowing vomit after inhaling substances.

Which drugs cause similar effects?

Most inhalants produce a rapid high that is similar to the effects of alcohol intoxication.

What is their legal status in the United States?

The common household products that are misused as inhalants are legally available for their intended and legitimate uses. Many state legislatures have attempted to deter youth who buy legal products to get high by placing restriction on the sale of these products to minors.

XII. Drugs of Concern

Even though some substances are not currently controlled by the Controlled Substances Act, they pose risks to individuals who abuse them. The following section describes these drugs of concern and their associated risks.

Bath Salts or Designer Cathinones
(Synthetic Stimulants)

WHAT ARE "BATH SALTS?"

Synthetic stimulants that are marketed as "bath salts" are often found in a number of retail products. These synthetic stimulants are chemicals. The chemicals are synthetic derivatives of cathinone, a central nervous system stimulant, which is an active chemical found naturally in the khat plant. Mephedrone and MDPV (3-4 methylenedioxypyrovalerone) are two of the designer cathinones most commonly found in these "bath salt" products. Many of these products are sold over the Internet, in convenience stores, and in "head shops."

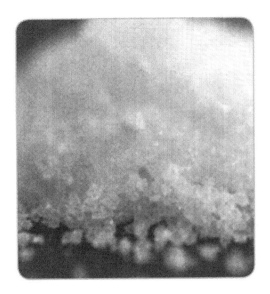

Bath salts

WHAT IS THEIR ORIGIN?

Law enforcement officials believe that the stimulant chemicals contained in these products are manufactured in China and India and packaged for wholesale distribution in Eastern Europe. Many countries have banned these products.

What are common street names?
→ Bilss, Blue Silk, Cloud Nine, Drone, Energy-1, Ivory Wave, Lunar Wave, Meow Meow, Ocean Burst, Pure Ivory, Purple Wave, Red Dove, Snow Leopard, Stardust, Vanilla Sky, White Dove, White Knight, White Lightening

What does it look like?
"Bath salt" stimulant products are sold in powder form in small plastic or foil packages of 200 and 500 milligrams under various brand names. Mephedrone is a fine white, off-white, or slightly yellow-colored powder. It can also be found in tablet and capsule form. MDPV is a fine white or off-white powder.

How is it abused?

"Bath salts" are usually ingested by sniffing/snorting. They can also be taken orally, smoked, or put into a solution and injected into veins.

What is their effect on the mind?

People who abuse these substances have reported agitation, insomnia, irritability, dizziness, depression, paranoia, delusions, suicidal thoughts, seizures, and panic attacks. Users have also reported effects including impaired perception of reality, reduced motor control, and decreased ability to think clearly.

What is their effect on the body?

Cathinone derivatives act as central nervous system stimulants causing rapid heart rate (which may lead to heart attacks and strokes), chest pains, nosebleeds, sweating, nausea, and vomiting.

What are their overdose effects?

These substances are usually marketed with the warning "not intended for human consumption." Any time that users put uncontrolled or unregulated substances into their bodies, the effects are unknown and can be dangerous.

Which drugs cause similar effects?

→ Amphetamine, Cocaine, Khat, LSD, MDMA

What is their legal status in the United States?

Mephedrone has no approved medical use in the United States. It is not specifically scheduled under the Controlled Substances Act, but it is a chemical analogue of methcathinone, which is a Schedule I controlled substance. Incidents involving mephedrone can be prosecuted under the Federal Analog Act of the Controlled Substances Act. MDPV (3,4-methylenedioxypyrovalerone) has no approved medical use in the United States. MDPV is not scheduled under the CSA.

DXM

WHAT IS DXM?

DXM is a cough suppressor found in more than 120 over-the-counter (OTC) cold medications, either alone or in combination with other drugs such as analgesics (e.g., acetaminophen), antihistamines (e.g., chlorpheniramine), decongestants (e.g., pseudoephedrine), and/or expectorants (e.g., guaifenesin). The typical adult dose for cough is 15 or 30 mg taken three to four times daily. The cough-suppressing effects of DXM persist for 5 to 6 hours after ingestion. When taken as directed, side-effects are rarely observed.

WHAT IS ITS ORIGIN?

DXM abusers can obtain the drug at almost any pharmacy or supermarket, seeking out the products with the highest concentration of the drug from among all the OTC cough and cold remedies that contain it. DXM products and powder can also be purchased on the Internet.

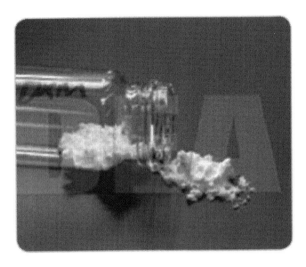

DXM powder

What are common street names?

Common street names include:

→ CCC, Dex, DXM, Poor Man's PCP, Robo, Rojo, Skittles, Triple C, and Velvet

What does it look like?

DXM can come in the form of:

→ Cough syrup, tablets, capsules, or powder

How is it abused?

DXM is abused in high doses to experience euphoria and visual and auditory hallucinations. Abusers take various amounts depending on their body weight and the effect they are attempting to achieve. Some abusers ingest 250 to 1,500 milligrams in a single dosage, far more than the recommended therapeutic dosages described above.

Illicit use of DXM is referred to on the street as "Robo-tripping," "skittling," or "dexing." The first two terms are derived from the products that are most commonly abused, Robitussin and Coricidin HBP. DXM abuse has traditionally involved drinking large volumes of the OTC liquid cough preparations. More recently, however, abuse of tablet and gel capsule preparations has increased.

These newer, high-dose DXM products have particular appeal for abusers. They are much easier to consume, eliminate the need to drink large volumes of unpleasant-tasting syrup, and are easily portable and concealed, allowing an abuser to continue to abuse DXM throughout the day, whether at school or work.

DXM powder, sold over the Internet, is also a source of DXM for abuse. (The powdered form of DXM poses additional risks to the abuser due to the uncertainty of composition and dose.)

DXM is also distributed in llicitly manufactured tablets containing only DXM or mixed with other drugs such as pseudoephedrine and/or methamphetamine.

DXM is abused by individuals of all ages, but its abuse by teenagers and young adults is of particular concern. This abuse is fueled by DXM's OTC availability and extensive "how to" abuse information on various web sites.

What is its effect on the mind?

Some of the many psychoactive effects associated with high-dose DXM include:

→ Confusion, inappropriate laughter, agitation, paranoia, and hallucinations

Other sensory changes, including the feeling of floating and changes in hearing and touch

Long-term abuse of DXM is associated with severe psychological dependence. Abusers of DXM describe the following four dose-dependent "plateaus":

PLATEAU	DOSE (MG)	BEHAVIORAL EFFECTS
1st	100 - 200	Mild stimulation
2nd	200 - 400	Euphoria and hallucinations
3rd	300 - 600	Distorted visual perceptions Loss of motor coordination
4th	500 - 1500	Out-of-body sensations

What is its effect on the body?

DXM intoxication involves:

→ Over-excitability, lethargy, loss of coordination, slurred speech, sweating, hypertension, and involuntary spasmodic movement of the eyeballs

The use of high doses of DXM in combination with alcohol or other drugs is particularly dangerous, and deaths have been reported. Approximately 5-10% of Caucasians are poor DXM metabolizers and at increased risk for overdoses and deaths. DXM taken with antidepressants can be life threatening.

OTC products that contain DXM often contain other ingredients such as acetaminophen, chlorpheniramine, and guaifenesin that have their own effects, such as:

→ Liver damage, rapid heart rate, lack of coordination, vomiting, seizures, and coma

To circumvent the many side effects associated with these other ingredients, a simple chemical extraction procedure has been developed and published on the Internet that removes most of these other ingredients in cough syrup.

What are its overdose effects?

DXM overdose can be treated in an emergency room setting and generally does not result in severe medical consequences or death. Most DXM-related deaths are caused by ingesting the drug in combination with other drugs. DXM-related deaths also occur from impairment of the senses, which can lead to accidents.

In 2003, a 14-year-old boy in Colorado who abused DXM died when he was hit by two cars as he attempted to cross a highway. State law enforcement investigators suspect that the drug affected the boy's depth perception and caused him to misjudge the distance and speed of the oncoming vehicles.

Which drugs cause similar effects?

Depending on the dose, DXM can have effects similar to marijuana or Ecstasy. In high doses its out-of-body effects are similar to those of Ketamine or PCP.

What is its legal status in the United States?

DXM is a legally marketed cough suppressant that is neither a controlled substance nor a regulated chemical under the Controlled Substances Act.

Salvia Divinorum

WHAT IS SALVIA DIVINORUM?

Salvia divinorum is a perennial herb in the mint family that is abused for its hallucinogenic effects.

WHAT IS ITS ORIGIN?

Salvia is native to certain areas of the Sierra Mazaleca region of Oaxaca, Mexico. It is one of several plants that are used by Mazatec Indians for ritual divination. Salvia divinorum plants can be grown successfully outside of this region. They can be grown indoors and outdoors, especially in humid semitropical climates.

What are common street names?

Common street names include:

→ Maria Pastora, Sally-D, and Salvia

What does it look like?

The plant has spade-shaped variegated green leaves that look similar to mint. The plants themselves grow to more than three feet high, have large green leaves, hollow square stems, and white flowers with purple calyces.

How is it abused?

Salvia can be chewed, smoked, or vaporized.

What is its effect on the mind?

Psychic effects include perceptions of bright lights, vivid colors, shapes, and body movement, as well as body or object distortions. Salvia divinorum may also cause fear and panic, uncontrollable laughter, a sense of overlapping realities, and hallucinations.

Salvinorin A is believed to be the ingredient responsible for the psychoactive effects of Salvia divinorum.

What is its effect on the body?

Adverse physical effects may include:

→ Loss of coordination, dizziness, and slurred speech

What are its overdose effects?

Adverse physical effects may include lack of coordination, dizziness, and slurred speech.

Which drugs cause similar effects?

When Salvia divinorum is chewed or smoked, the hallucinogenic effects elicited are similar to those induced by other Schedule I hallucinogenic substances.

What is its legal status in the United States?

Neither Salvia divinorum nor its active constituent Salvinorin A has an approved medical use in the United States. Salvia is not controlled under the Controlled Substances Act. Salvia divinorum is, however, controlled by a number of states. Since Salvia is not controlled by the CSA, some online botanical companies and drug promotional sites have advertised Salvia as a legal alternative to other plant hallucinogens like mescaline.

Leaves of the salvia divinorum plant

XIII. Resources

DRUG PREVENTION RESOURCES

Drug prevention programs are designed and implemented on many levels. The federal government has instituted a number of national drug prevention programs which reach targeted populations through public service announcements, grant programs, educational programs and the sharing of expertise. State and local governments also have a significant number of prevention programs which are tailored to address particular problems and needs. Law enforcement and the military have brought drug prevention expertise into classrooms and communities; businesses have also contributed significantly to drug prevention through sponsored programs, drug-free policies and corporate support for community initiatives. Other segments of society, including faith-based institutions, civic organizations, and private foundations are also active forces in drug prevention.

Below is a partial list of drug prevention agencies and programs. There are many other outstanding efforts which are ongoing across the nation; it is impossible to include them all. Some programs are aimed at particular populations or specific drugs. Within a given agency, there may be many prevention programs which are aimed at different audiences.

FEDERAL DRUG PREVENTION AGENCIES AND PROGRAMS:

Drug Enforcement Administration (DEA):
In addition to dismantling the major drug trafficking organizations, DEA is committed to reducing the demand for drugs in America. DEA's Demand Reduction Program is carried out by Special Agents across the United States who work in communities to share expertise and information on drug trends, emerging problems, and the dangers of drugs.

→ www.dea.gov
→ www.JustThinkTwice.com
→ www.GetSmartAboutDrugs.com

Office of National Drug Control Policy (ONDCP):
This office reports to the President of the United States. ONDCP administers the Youth Anti-Drug Media Campaign.

→ www.mediacampaign.org
→ www.whitehousedrugpolicy.gov

Substance Abuse and Mental Health Services Administration (SAMHSA):
This organization is responsible for overseeing and administering mental health, drug prevention, and drug treatment programs around the nation. The Center for Substance Abuse Prevention (CSAP) and the Center for Substance Abuse Treatment (CSAT) are part of SAMHSA.

→ www.samhsa.gov
→ www.samhsa.gov/prevention
→ www.samhsa.gov/about/csap.aspx

U.S. Department of Education (ED):
ED has many anti-drug programs.
→ www.ed.gov

National Institute on Drug Abuse (NIDA):
NIDA conducts and disseminates the results of research about the effects of drugs on the body and the brain. NIDA is an excellent source of information on drug addiction.
→ www.nida.nih.gov

National Guard:
The National Guard provides drug education to communities in all 50 states.
→ www.ngb.army.mil

Weed and Seed:

Operation Weed and Seed is a strategy to prevent and reduce violent crime, drug abuse, and gang activity in targeted high-crime neighborhood. Law enforcement agencies and prosecutors cooperate in "weeding out" criminals and "seeding" to bring in human services, prevention intervention, treatment, and neighborhood revitalization.

→ www.ojp.usdoj.gov/ccdo/ws/welcome.html

Other Anti-Drug Organizations:

National Association of State Alcohol and Drug Abuse Directors (NASADAD)
→ www.nasadad.org

Community Anti-Drug Coalitions Of America (CADCA)
→ www.cadca.org

National Crime Prevention Council (NCPC)
→ www.ncpc.org

National Families in Action (NFIA)
→ www.nationalfamilies.org

You can obtain free anti-drug information from:

National Clearinghouse for Alcohol and Drug Information (NCADI)
→ www.health.org

The National Center on Addiction and Substance Abuse at Columbia University (CASA)
→ www.casacolumbia.org

Elks Drug Awareness Program
→ www.elks.org/dap

Partnership for a Drug-Free America (PDFA)
→ www.drugfree.org

Scott Newman Center
→ www.scottnewmancenter.org

American Council for Drug Education (ACDE)
→ www.acde.org

Drug Strategies
→ www.drugstrategies.org

Youth Anti-Drug Organizations:

Learning For Life
→ www.learning-for-life.org

PRIDE Youth Programs
→ www.prideyouthprograms.org

Drug Abuse Resistance Education (DARE America) (DARE)
→ www.dare.com

Students Against Destructive Decisions (SADD)
→ www.sadd.org

Law Enforcement Exploring
→ www.learning-for-life.org/exploring/lawenforcement/